Dear Clarissa,
Best of luck!!
Andy Brick
6-24-10

EXPLORING CULTURE

EXPLORING CULTURE:

How to do Business with 17 Cultural and Religious Groups

Building a Bridge to Understanding

by

Andrew Erlich, Ph. D.

Multi-Cultural Publications
Paradise Valley, Arizona

Requests for permission or further information
should be addressed to:

Permissions Department,
MULTI-CULTURAL PUBLICATIONS
5201 E. Hatcher Road
Paradise Valley, AZ 85253

Multi-Cultural Publications
is a division of
Erlich Transcultural Consultants

ISBN 978-0-9774089-1-7

Designed by Book Group, Las Vegas NV
Cover designed by Jim Piper, Los Angeles CA

Printed in U.S.A.

INTRODUCTION

Diversity, multiculturalism, globalization . . . as we continue to grow and encounter people of multiple backgrounds and ethnicities, these one-time buzzwords are fast becoming a permanent part of our national lexicon. While our different ways of life are continuously integrating and influencing each other, lack of knowledge often can inhibit successful communication across cultures.

This book provides a very important first step in providing the knowledge necessary for success when doing business across cultures. Our goal is to present to you important background information on some of the major ethnic groups that are present in the United States. You might note the absence of certain groups. Although each and every group is important, it was beyond the scope of this publication to include all groups. However, we have attempted to provide you with the information that is most relevant for your business. Each chapter includes a brief summary for quick reference, the latest demographics, pertinent cultural insights, business dos and don'ts, financial information, a brief historical background, information on religion, important holidays and language, as well as specific information on the market.

We have attempted to provide you with what are called "valid cultural assumptions", which, unlike stereotypes, leave ample room for individual differences. The words on the following pages are not set in stone and are not meant to place judgment or value on any one set of behaviors over another. Our purpose is simply to help you gain a better understanding of the values, norms, beliefs and behaviors common to a particular group of people, as well as to provide you with some of the historical forces that might have shaped them. We warn, however, that the information in this book should not be considered a cultural "recipe book" to be applied to every individual within an ethnic or religious group. Diverse subcultures can exist within each group; and while individuals often share many commonalities, there are also significant differences among them based on factors like personality, gender, generation, economic status and level of acculturation.

The purpose of this book is to provide a foundation that will help you overcome the mistakes that can hinder communication across cultures. Ultimately, effective communication depends on your ability to recognize how your own culture has shaped your worldview and your subsequent assumptions about other people, your willingness to listen and learn from people who are different from yourself, and patience. We hope this book will not only improve your business efforts, but also give you greater insight into the cultural richness that surrounds you.

Andrew Erlich, Ph.D.
January, 2008

Acknowledgments

This update of our 2002 book has been a collaborative project. In addition to the original writing staff, I would like to thank Huafu Jiang, Joan Lawton, Laura Mitre and Sonya Hemmings for their overall editing and updating of this project.

Special thanks should be given to those individuals who originally took the time to help us proof and edit each chapter: Tami Ekizian, Esq., Dr. Karen Gunn, Faisal Maju, Sang H. Choi, Sung Yul Jung, Hojiu Song, Susan Song, Akiko Ikehara, Kiko Ruben, Randy Aleman, Steven Reich, Shirley James, Anh Do, Dr. Brian Leung, Enrico Obusan, Dr. Edmundo Litton, Max Song, Dr. Purnima Chawla, Ravi Singh, Rabbi Howard Simon, Harry and Myra Morewitz, and Victor Danilin.

.

Terminology and Ethnic Identification

Latino and Hispanic

We are often asked, "What is the best, most appropriate and most respectful name to use in describing this population?"
- Latino
- Hispanic
- Mexican-American, Cuban-American, Puerto Rican, Dominican, etc.?

The simple answer is that it depends on to whom you are talking. Individuals choose to state their ethnic identification in many different ways: sometimes geographically or by national origin and sometimes politically (Chicanos, Boriquas).

Latino

The terms *Latino* (male) and *Latina* (female) refer to an individual who was born in or whose family originated in Latin America. Many prefer Latino to the term Hispanic because it excludes Europeans and reinforces their origin in civilizations that predated the Spanish Conquest or because it is a Spanish word. In our research, we have found that the term Latino is popular in California, New York, New Jersey and Illinois.

Hispanic

The term *Hispanic* is frequently used as well. The U.S. government first coined this English-language term for use in the 1970 census. It is a word that, for many, elicits a strong connection with Latin Americans' Spanish heritage. We have found this term to be popular in Texas and Florida.

Chicano

Chicano was originally considered to be a derogatory term. As the story goes, it had its origins in the fields of California in the 1930s. Indigenous Mexican migrant farm workers whose pronunciation of Spanish was influenced by their native Nahuatl language described themselves as "Mesheecanos" as opposed to "Mexicanos". Things that were associated with or directly connected to Mexico's indigenous past were viewed negatively, as a source of and connection to the humiliation of the Spanish Conquest and the subsequent "rape" of Latin America. Thus, this term became derogatory until the 1960s, when it was embraced by the "Brown Power" movement. These young Latinos embraced this term as an affirmation of their connection with their indigenous heritage. Currently, the term has negative connotations for some Latinos who view it as having a connection with radical activism. Others view it with pride as a symbol of the fight for civil rights.

Boriqua

Borinquén is the indigenous (Taìno) name for the island that would be called Puerto Rico by the Spanish. The residents of this island were called *Boriqua*. This word's use has several implications. For one, it can imply a political choice to connect to a Spanish-speaking Latin American reality and identity as opposed to an English-speaking United States reality and identity. It is also commonly used as a term of endearment among Puerto Ricans.

Overall, the secret in what to call an individual is to ask what he or she prefers.

Asian vs. Oriental

As with Latinos, once the many different people who make up the countries of Asia arrive in the United States, they are often lumped together in the umbrella group "Asians". The term "Asian" or "Asian American" originated in the highly politicized climate of the late 1960s and 1970s, when Asian American activists sought to end the usage of the term "Oriental".

Although both terms are rooted in geography, *Asian* is usually considered neutral. *Oriental*, on the other hand, is often considered offensive. This term, which means "of or situated in the East", refers to countries and peoples in terms of their location relative to Europe. More importantly, however, the term refers back to the days of Western colonialism and connotes images of exoticism and barbarism. While Oriental is still used as an adjective describing inanimate objects (i.e., Oriental rugs), it has been deemed inappropriate when referring to people. The term *Asian* has become the norm, but if possible, it is always better to refer to a person by their immediate ethnic/national group.

Black and African American

Terminology referring to American Blacks also has changed with the times. In the post-Civil War era, the term *Black*, along with *Negro*, was considered offensive to emancipated slaves and their descendants, who preferred the term *colored*. A capitalized *Negro* was embraced by the community and replaced *colored* in the early 20th century. The Black Power movement of the 1960s, however, called on the community to embrace the term *Black* as a term of racial pride. *Afro-American* also gained popularity in the 1960s and 1970s as a term that expressed a growing pride in Black heritage. Ramona H. Edelin, president of the National Urban Coalition, and the Rev. Jesse Jackson popularized the term *African American* in the late 1980s. *African American* is widely accepted today, and is the most appropriate term to use in public discourse. There is still a strong in-group preference, however, for *Black*.

TABLE OF CONTENTS

African Americans

African Americans:
SUMMARY

Demographics

- In 2005, there were 36.8 million African Americans in the U.S., comprising approximately 13 percent of the total population.
- The five states most populated by African Americans are New York, Florida, Georgia, Texas and California.

Cultural Insights

- Many African Americans might express that they live in two separate worlds (Black and White) and must change their behaviors in each.
- There is a strong sense of community among African Americans.
- Family is extremely important among African Americans. This culture also emphasizes respect for elders in the community and tends to be child-centric.
- The majority of African Americans are liberal Democrats. Some are more conservative about certain social issues, such as abortion and homosexuality. This is likely tied to the importance of religion within the community.
- Ceremony (i.e., graduations, weddings, retirement) is important among African Americans.
- In the professional workplace, African American employees tend to be excluded from the informal social networks and connections that are crucial for success.
- A Black person responding passionately to what might seem to be a small discriminatory act is not being hypersensitive. Behind that response are decades of racial discrimination and insensitivity.
- While African Americans celebrate the holidays of mainstream America, certain holidays, like Martin Luther King Jr. Day, Juneteenth, and Kwanzaa are especially significant to many in the African American community.

Business Practices: Dos and Don'ts

Dos

- Be genuine.
- Always be aware of what you are saying and doing while conducting business with clients. Some stereotypes and negative attitudes are so deeply embedded that they can be expressed half-consciously or unconsciously with African Americans as well as with people of other cultures.

Don'ts

- Don't make assumptions based on dress or hairstyle.

- It is never appropriate to use the words "nigger", "colored", or "Negro", even if you are joking with friends, and even if they use the term among one another.
- Always avoid any kind of racial jokes.
- Never talk down to or patronize anyone.
- Attempt to get to know your Black customers and associates on a personal level.
- No matter how experienced and able Black businesspeople are, they are often subject to the automatic assumption that their products and services are inferior.

African Americans

Demographics

In 2005, the African American population of the United States numbered 36.8 million, or approximately 13 percent of the total population.

Most Blacks reside in the South (55 percent). Seventeen percent live in the Northeast, 19 percent in the Midwest and 10 percent in the West.

The 10 most African American populated states in 2005 were:

1. New York (2,858,065)
2. Florida (2,613,628)
3. Georgia (2,571,396)
4. Texas (2,442,350)
5. California (2,163,530)
6. Illinois (1,803,613)
7. North Carolina (1,765,698)
8. Maryland (1,564,914)
9. Louisiana (1,425,685)
10. Virginia (1,397,192)

The top 10 African American markets in 2005 were:

1. New York (2,011,962)
2. Chicago (943,752)
3. Detroit (686,241)
4. Philadelphia (628,312)
5. Houston (455,764)
6. Memphis, Tenn. (404,970)
7. Baltimore (396,495)
8. Los Angeles (368,711)
9. New Orleans (295,259)
10. Washington DC (292,445)

Cultural Insights

Worldview

- African Americans attach significant importance to freedom, justice and equality.

- A history of struggle and discrimination shapes the African American worldview.

- There is a strong sense of community among African Americans. When injustice befalls an African American, it is felt by the community. At the same time, the entire community can take pride in the achievements of one Black person. There is also a sense that once someone has "made it", they owe it to their community to help others. In situations where African Americans are not the majority, this sense of community often manifests itself in some form of mutual recognition (i.e., a nod of the head or a smile)—verbal or nonverbal.

- Family, both nuclear and extended, is extremely important among African Americans. There is also much respect for elders in the community. African American culture tends to be child-centric, meaning that children and their needs are considered priorities.

Sense of Self

- Past and present experiences have forced African Americans to base their identity on their racial heritage. Attached to this is a strong sense of community and history.

- Some African Americans might express that they have to maintain a sort of "double consciousness", or the feeling that they live in two separate worlds (Black and White) and must change their behaviors in each.

- For some, status is important, as well as physical signs of that status. Status symbols tend to provide a measure of value and worth in a society where, for so long, African Americans were devalued.

Sense of Space

- For African Americans, sense of space is negotiated and reduced over time as comfort and familiarity increase. Remain formal until you receive indication that a less formal stance is acceptable.

Communication Style

- African Americans are more likely to be direct and not as resistant to assertion as the mainstream population. This is often misinterpreted as an expression of aggression.

- Some African Americans tend to be more comfortable with expressive verbal communication. Many might utilize a broader spectrum of nonverbal behaviors (e.g., tone and volume of voice). However, not all ascribe to this behavior.

Eye Contact

- Direct eye contact is important. Lack of direct eye contact when listening to an individual speaking, however, is not an indication of a lack of attention.

Language

- The variety of accents among African Americans reflects the great diversity of the population. Accents range from northern, southern and Midwestern U.S. to Caribbean, African and European.

- The switching of dialects, depending on the person being addressed, is not uncommon among African Americans.

Time and Time Consciousness

- African Americans tend to be more flexible and relaxed with time than is common in mainstream America.

Values and Norms

- Education is important within the African American community. This is evident in the fact that increased numbers of Blacks have obtained bachelor and advanced degrees.

- Hard work is a norm within the African American community. African Americans often feel they have to overachieve to prove their worth in White, majority environments.

- In general, the African American community is religious. African Americans tend to be more expressive of their spirituality than is common in mainstream America.

- The majority of African Americans are liberal Democrats. Some are more conservative about certain social issues, such as abortion and homosexuality. This is likely tied to the importance of religion within the community.

- Ceremony is important among African Americans. There is a great respect for graduations, weddings, retirements, etc., and many, especially those in older generations, prefer for these ceremonies to be traditional.

Business Practices: Dos and Don'ts

Dos

- Attempt to get to know your customers and/or associates on a personal level.

- Be genuine. It is not necessary to make comments concerning race matters in an effort to relate to your African American associate.

- Always be aware of what you are saying and doing while conducting business with African American clients. Some stereotypes and negative attitudes are so deeply embedded that they can be expressed half-consciously or unconsciously with African Americans as well as with people from other cultures (i.e., you might be thinking in racial terms when choosing a neighborhood, business partner, employees, etc.). A Black person responding passionately to what might seem to be a small discriminatory act is not being hypersensitive. Behind that response are decades of racial discrimination and insensitivity.

Don'ts

- Don't make assumptions based on dress or hairstyle. African American professionals often complain that some treat them differently when they are dressed more casually.

- It is never appropriate to use the words "nigger", "colored", or "negro", even if you are joking with friends, and even if African Americans use them among one another.

- Always avoid any kind of racial jokes.

- Never talk down to or patronize anyone. Don't assume your customers are unaware of what you are talking about.

- Don't assume that because someone did not attend a well-known college or university that his/her education is below par.

- Don't make assumptions on the quality of a product or service. No matter how able and experienced, Black businesspeople are often subject to the automatic assumption that their products and services are inferior.

Historical Background

It is estimated that between 1502 and 1860, approximately 10 million to 20 million African slaves were transported to the New World. Less than half survived the trip. The majority were taken to the Caribbean, Brazil or the Spanish colonies of Central and South America. Only about 6 percent were traded in British North America. The first African slaves brought to the English colonies in North America came on a Dutch privateer that landed at Jamestown, Virginia, in August 1619.

By 1750, there were nearly 240,000 people of African descent in North America. After the American Revolution, northern states began to abolish slavery. By the 1820s, virtually all slaves in the United States were in the South, where the slave trade thrived with the booming cotton economy. Northern abolitionist movements gained ground in the 1830s, and often joined forces with Black organizations in their battles to end slavery.

More than 200,000 Blacks served during the Civil War. In 1863, President Abraham Lincoln signed the Emancipation Proclamation, freeing slaves held by southerners. With the war's end in 1865, the 13th Amendment that formally abolished slavery was ratified. Although the Freedmen's Bureau was established to aid freed slaves, southern states established Black codes to restrict Black land ownership. Eventually, the 14th Amendment (guaranteeing citizenship to Blacks), as well as the Reconstruction Act, were passed. The federal military occupied the South, and the 15th Amendment was passed, giving Black men the right to vote. Blacks advanced politically, but southern Democrats used violence to keep Blacks away from the polls and to restrict Black opportunities. Still, Blacks made some gains. Several Black colleges were founded in the late 1800s, as well as the first Black financial institutions.

In the early 20th century, Jim Crow segregation kept Blacks separate from Whites, while sharecropping kept them dependent on Whites. Southern Whites continued to develop ways to disenfranchise Blacks. For example, Blacks had to pass literacy tests and pay poll taxes in order to vote. In the 10 years between 1890 and 1900, more than 1,200 Blacks were lynched in the United States. Blacks responded differently to the discrimination. Booker T. Washington, for example, advocated racial accommodation and urged Blacks to acquire occupational skills for economic advancement. Groups led by people like W.E.B Du Bois demanded civil rights through political and social protest.

Growing unemployment, racial unrest and the need for wartime industrial labor encouraged Blacks to leave the South. From 1910 to 1930, between 1.5 million and 2 million African Americans left the South for the industrial cities of the North.

An increasing sense of racial pride and social cohesion began to develop. Black veterans returned to increasing prejudice and racial pride grew even more, as was evident during the period known

8

as the Harlem Renaissance. Blacks were devastated during the Great Depression. They lost their jobs at much higher rates than Whites and remained out of work longer. Roosevelt's New Deal had mixed results for Blacks. Relief programs provided aid, but segregation and unemployment continued. It was around this time that Black political support shifted from the Republican Party to the Democratic Party.

More than a million Blacks served in the armed forces during WWII, and Black migration continued north. The struggle against Hitler forced many Whites to re-evaluate their views on discrimination and spurred some to accept racial equality. In the late 1940s, Supreme Court rulings began to strike down many methods of discrimination. The United States became more embarrassed of its treatment of Blacks during the Cold War and continued progress was made. In 1954, the NAACP won *Brown* vs. *The Board of Education of Topeka*, declaring segregated facilities unequal and unconstitutional. Southerners utilized violent tactics to prevent integration to the point where federal troops were sent to enforce the law. Decades later, schools still remained virtually segregated.

The struggle for equal rights was energized by the Brown decision and further catalyzed by activists like Rosa Parks and Martin Luther King, Jr. Nonviolent movements and protests led by groups like the Southern Christian Leadership Conference (SCLC) brought the movement national attention. The Civil Rights Bill was passed in 1964. Disadvantage continued, however, and the Black power movement began to grow in the urban North. Violence erupted in urban areas during the 1960s. The Black Panther Party formed in Oakland, California.

Legal segregation ended during the 1960s, but segregation by custom continued. Generally, landlords in White neighborhoods would not rent to Black tenants; banks denied financing; and real estate agents refused to show houses in traditionally White areas to Blacks, even if they could afford them. Discriminatory hiring practices confined most Black workers to the least-secure, lowest-paying jobs—regardless of their qualifications. Those few opportunities open to Black professionals like doctors, lawyers and teachers were in positions and institutions serving the Black community. As a result of limited opportunities, more than half of African Americans had incomes below the poverty line by the beginning of the 1960s.

Anti-poverty programs were put in place and had positive effects: The Black middle class grew and Black unemployment shrank to less than 7 percent in 1968 and 1969. The contracting economy of the 1970s, however, provoked White opposition to programs that had benefited African Americans. White reaction to expanded Black economic and educational opportunities was often harsh. White protestors burned buses, harassed Black schoolchildren and supported local politicians who opposed Black equality. Republican President Richard M. Nixon turned away from civil rights. High unemployment continued through the Carter and Reagan years. Defense spending increased and governmental support for social programs dwindled. For African Americans, the consequences of these changes were alarming. By the end of the decade, the after-tax income of the richest 1 percent of Americans had increased by 87 percent, while the income of those at the bottom of the economy diminished. Black unemployment grew rapidly. In 1983, Black unemployment stood at a record high of almost 21 percent. By 1989, almost one-third of all Black Americans were below the poverty line—more than three times the rate for Whites. The income gap between Black and White Americans grew dramatically. The disparity between middle-class and working-class Blacks also grew during this period.

Despite obstacles, African Americans have made significant political and economic gains. While many Whites think that racial discrimination has declined to the point of nonexistence, Blacks tend to believe that more needs to be done to fight racial discrimination. Blatant and public displays of racial intolerance and violence are constant reminders that racial intolerance still exists.

Religion

Most African Americans practice some form of Protestantism. Protestantism's relatively loose hierarchical structure, particularly in the Baptist and Methodist denominations, has allowed African Americans to create and maintain separate churches that have enabled them to take up positions of leadership denied to them in mainstream America. In addition to their religious role, African American churches traditionally provide political leadership and serve social-welfare functions.

A significant number of African Americans are Black Muslims. In fact, approximately 45 percent of Muslims in the United States are African American. The most prominent Black Muslim group is the Nation of Islam, a religious organization founded by W. D. Fard and Elijah Poole in 1935. Poole, who changed his name to Elijah Muhammad, soon emerged as the leader of the Nation of Islam. Today, Louis Farrakhan leads the Nation of Islam. A small number of African American Muslims worship independently of the Nation of Islam, as part of the mainstream Islamic tradition.

There also has been an increase of African Americans shifting toward Pentecostalism, with significant leadership displayed by Bishop T.D. Jakes. By many accounts, Jakes' s ministry has surpassed that of mainstream national Protestant Evangelist Billy Graham in both popularity and size.

The African American Market

There is an increasing economic bifurcation, or polarization, among African Americans. On average, Black income is increasing. At the same time, there is more of a distance between lower and upper classes than is the norm for other groups. The earnings of educated African Americans are on the rise. Earnings of those with a high school education or less have declined, most likely due to an industrial complex that prefers cheaper, immigrant labor or sending jobs offshore. Each group faces discrimination in a different way. For those within lower income brackets, discrimination deals with more structural-level issues (i.e., less than adequate access to quality schooling).

Middle- and upper-class African Americans usually deal with racism on a more personal, interactive basis. For example, they are more likely to find themselves in an occupational situation in which they are the only Black person. This might lead to situations where they are under extreme scrutiny and feel they have to work harder to prove their ability, and where they might have to deal with assumptions that they represent their entire race, or beliefs that they are there to fill quotas.

Gender issues are often ignored in the African American community. Relationships between men and women, however, do not always follow the outline of mainstream White America.

10

Historically, Black women are more likely to have had to work outside of the home than non-Hispanic White women. In terms of education, more Black women received bachelor's degrees in 1999 than did Black men (16 percent to 14 percent). The reverse was true for non-Hispanic Whites (25 percent women vs. 31 percent men).

Degree of Acculturation

As mentioned above, the educational and occupational advances of the African American middle class have allowed for a small degree of economic assimilation within mainstream society. In the not-so-distant past, most African Americans were forced to live together in the same communities. The small, pre-integration middle class served the Black community only. More recently, economic separation often leads to physical separation between the classes. This, in turn, leads to a sort of social distancing. More importantly, incentives for Black solidarity are still extremely strong. Both groups have been touched by racism. Issues that involve blatant racist practices will bring them together. Most, no matter what class, would agree that efforts should be focused on empowering the "Black community."

Black immigrants are a group that is usually ignored among both African American groups and the U.S. population at large. Some first-generation immigrants attempt to dissassociate themselves from the African American community for fear of the negative steretypes associated with the group. It is not uncommon for later generations, however, to assimilate into the African American subculture.

Economic Status

Unemployment is higher among Blacks than Whites. The unemployment rate for Blacks is more than twice that of Whites. This is true for both men and women.

Black men are less likely than non-Hispanic White men to be employed in managerial and professional jobs. The proportion of White men in these types of professions is almost double that of Blacks. A similar trend is true for women. Within the professional workplace, African American employees tend to be excluded from the informal social networks and connections that are usually crucial for success. Black men and women are more likely to work in service occupations.

Single female-headed households are more likely to have lower incomes. In general, Black income is on the rise, but racial differences in wealth are still significant.

Holidays and Celebrations

African Americans celebrate the holidays of mainstream America. There are, however, specific holidays and celebrations of particular significance to the African American population.

Martin Luther King Day—Third Monday in January: "MLK Day" celebrates the life of civil rights activist Martin Luther King, Jr. and serves as a reminder of the civil rights struggle for African Americans. Many in Congress were opposed to the holiday. In the years leading up to the official decree as a holiday, many African Americans celebrated the birthday themselves—with a few states declaring King's birthday a state holiday. Many would not go to work or school on that day. The bill was finally passed by both the House of Representatives and the Senate and was signed into law on Nov. 2, 1983. The day is usually celebrated with parades and large convocations on the third Monday in January.

Black History Month—February: Black History Month (usually February) is set aside for people to focus on African American history and the contributions of African Americans in the United States. Black communities will often organize educational and cultural events throughout the month.

Juneteenth—June 19: Juneteenth is the oldest known celebration of the ending of slavery and dates back to 1865. It was on June 19 of that year that Union soldiers, led by Major General Gordon Granger, landed at Galveston, Texas, with news that the war had ended and that the enslaved were now free. Note that this was two-and-a-half years after President Lincoln's Emancipation Proclamation, which had become official Jan. 1, 1863. Juneteenth celebrations are growing in popularity. They are now most popular in Texas (where Juneteenth is celebrated as a state holiday).

The Black Family Reunion: Many African American families have annual or biennial family reunions during the summer months. These events tend to be quite large (numbers of attendees can be in the 100s) and well organized. Family members from all over the country will travel to one location for several days to celebrate and learn more about their family history with organized events and banquets. Some families are so organized that committee members meet monthly to plan the annual event.

Christmas—Dec. 25: Besides being an important Christian holiday, Christmas was often the only day during the year that southern Black slaves did not have to work.

Kwanzaa—Dec. 26-Jan. 1: Dr. Maulana Karenga—professor and chair of the Department of Black Studies at California State University, Long Beach—created Kwanzaa in 1966. It is an African American and Pan-African holiday, the purpose of which is to celebrate family, community and culture. The holiday's origins are in the first harvest celebrations of Africa. The name Kwanzaa is derived from the phrase *matunda ya kwanza*, which means "first fruits" in Swahili. The meaning of Kwanzaa is based on Seven Principles rooted in African communitarian philosophy. The seven principles are *umoja* (unity), *kujichagulia* (self-determination), *ujima* (collective work and responsibility), *ujamaa* (cooperative economics), *nia* (purpose), *kuumba* (creativity), and *imani* (faith). On each of the seven days of Kwanzaa, the family comes together around a traditionally decorated table and lights a candle corresponding to the principle for that day. That principle is then discussed and a commitment is made to promote that principle throughout the year.

Jumping the Broom (wedding tradition): Slaves were not allowed to marry legally. However, they held their own ceremonies that included the couple jumping over a broom to signify that they were married. Today, many African Americans include jumping the broom within the traditional wedding ceremony.

NOTES

Armenian Americans

Armenian Americans:
SUMMARY

Demographics

- There were approximately 421,000 people of Armenian ancestry in the United States in 2005. Some estimate the current number is closer to 500,000 or 1,000,000.
- Los Angeles contains the largest Armenian population outside Armenia. It is estimated that 171,000 (41 percent) Armenians reside in the Los Angeles region, although the number is, most likely, much higher.

Cultural Insights

- The "ian" at the end of a surname is a sign of Armenian descent and identity.
- *Hye* is a term used by insiders for Armenian. *Odar* means foreigner or outsider.
- The experience of oppression by the Ottoman Turks in the 19th and early 20th centuries is an extremely important and unifying point in history for Armenian groups. Especially important is the Armenian holocaust of 1914-15, carried out by Turkey.
- Animosity continues between Armenian and Turkish immigrants in the United States.
- Years of foreign rule and victimization of Armenia and the resulting Armenian Diaspora create a deep sense of cultural loss among Armenians.
- The family is at the center of Armenian culture.
- More traditional families tend to be highly patriarchal, and gender roles are clear.
- When possible, many Armenians prefer to support Armenian businesses and deal with Armenian businesspeople.
- Armenian immigrants tend to be price-conscious and are willing to shop around to find a bargain.
- Armenians often look down upon wastefulness.
- An important holiday among Armenian Americans is the observance of Genocide Memorial Day.

Business Practices: Dos and Don'ts

Dos

- Be aware that the Armenian Diaspora includes people from Middle Eastern and Arab countries, the former Soviet Armenia and Armenia. Certain cultural and business practices might be particular to the specific country of origin.
- Be on time, but don't be surprised if your Armenian associate is a little late. Patience is considered a virtue. Allow plenty of time for each appointment.

Don'ts

- Do not be discouraged by belated replies to inquiries, letters and faxes, or by the lack of a reply.

Armenian Americans

Demographics

The most recent census data estimate that there were a little more than 421,000 people of Armenian descent in the United States in 2005. Others claim, however, that census data are skewed and that a more accurate count would find somewhere between a half-million to 1 million Armenians in this country. Many are now members of the third and fourth generations on American soil.

The top Armenian markets in the United States are:

1. Los Angeles
2. Boston
3. Chicago
4. Fresno CA
5. New York
6. Philadelphia
7. Providence RI
8. San Francisco
9. Washington DC

According to the Census American Community Survey in 2005, 55 percent (232,480) of Armenians are in California. Los Angeles County contains the largest Armenian population outside of Armenia. Approximately 171,000 (41 percent) of Armenian Americans were living in the Los Angeles region in 2005 (although insider estimates claim more than 200,000).

Cultural Insights

Worldview

- The family is at the center of Armenian culture. Family and group needs take precedence over individual needs. Great respect is given to elders. Unmarried youth will often live with family members until marriage, and married couples often remain close to family.

- The years of foreign rule and victimization of Armenia and the resulting Armenian Diaspora created a deep sense of cultural loss among Armenians. The impact of this reality is often perceived as a loss of Armenian cultural development and cultural unity, as well as the death of an ancient culture.

Sense of Self

- Armenian identity and pride are largely based in a common history of struggle and oppression. Even though younger generations might not have experienced oppression firsthand, Armenian history remains central to their identity. The experience of oppression by the Ottoman Turks in the 19th and early 20th centuries is an especially important and unifying point in history for Armenian groups. During the Armenian holocaust of 1914-15 by Turkey, it is estimated that between 600,000 and 1.5 million

18

Armenians died at the hands of the Turkish government. Present generations continue to feel victimized, largely because the Turkish government still denies that the event ever took place. There is still animosity between Armenian and Turkish immigrants in the United States. Even Armenian youth will often have deeply felt ill feelings toward Turks. While North Americans are knowledgeable about the Jewish Holocaust, there is little awareness in this country of the Armenian genocide.

- Group identity is central to the Armenian sense of self. For example, *Hye* is a term used by insiders for Armenian. *Odar* means foreigner or outsider. One can be *Hye* by blood, or increasingly outsiders (such as non-Armenian spouses) can become *Hye* by learning and using the Armenian language, attending the Armenian Church or sharing common sentiments with Armenians. Those who are not Armenian by blood or marriage are not considered for membership into the Armenian Apostolic Church or the organized community.

Sense of Space

- Armenians are comfortable speaking at closer distances than mainstream Americans.

Communication Style

- Armenians are generally quite expressive. They might talk with their hands and speak at a high volume.

- It is often important for Armenians that their opinions be heard and considered.

Eye Contact

- In general, rules of eye contact are similar to those in mainstream culture. Be aware, however, that rules might change depending on the country of origin of the individual.

Language

- Armenians are proud to have developed their own language. The Armenian language (Hayeren) is a separate Indo-European tongue sharing some phonetic and grammatical features with other Caucasian languages, such as Georgian. The Iranian languages contributed many words related to cultural subjects, but the majority of the Armenian word stock shows no connection with other existing languages. Some experts believe this derives from extinct non-Indo-European languages. The distinct alphabet of 38 letters, derived from the Greek alphabet, has existed since the early fifth century A.D.

- Classical Armenian is used today only in religious ceremonies. Modern, spoken Armenian is divided into a number of dialects, the most important of which are the eastern dialect (used in Armenia, the rest of Transcaucasia and Iran) and the western dialect (used extensively in Turkey and among Western émigrés).

- About 60 percent of Armenian Americans have the ability to speak Armenian. It would not be surprising, however, if this estimate is a little low. According to the census, only about

28 percent are unable to speak English "very well".

- Many Armenian children go to Armenian schools and are forced to speak Armenian at home. Most are bilingual.

- Armenian dialects can differ depending on the person's region of origin.

Time and Time Consciousness

- Armenian culture is more relaxed and laid back than mainstream U.S. culture regarding time.

- Punctuality is not always considered a value among Armenian groups. This is especially true for social occasions, but less true in professional and business situations.

Values and Norms

- Education is highly valued among Armenians.

- The importance of education is combined with the importance of maintaining ethnic ties and identity. For example, many Armenian churches have founded their own schools.

- Armenian youth, for the most part—even those born in the United States—are made aware of Armenian politics, current affairs, culture and religious practices.

- In-group ties are strong. Parents prefer that their children marry within the Armenian population.

- The "ian" at the end of a surname is a sign of Armenian descent and identity. In the 1920s and 30s, many Armenian Americans changed their names to avoid discrimination or because the names were considered difficult to pronounce for North Americans. Today name-changing is a less common occurrence, although some Armenian Americans will still shorten their first names.

- More traditional families tend to be highly patriarchal, and gender roles are clear. More Americanized youth have a greater tendency to break with traditional roles.

- When possible, Armenians prefer to support Armenian businesses and deal with Armenian businesspeople.

- Armenian immigrants tend to be price-conscious and are willing to shop around for bargains.

- Armenians often look down upon wastefulness.

Business Practices: Dos and Don'ts

Dos

- Be aware that the Armenian Diaspora includes people from Middle Eastern and Arab countries, the former Soviet Armenia and Armenia. Certain cultural and business

20

practices might be particular to the specific country of origin.

- Be on time, but don't be surprised if your Armenian associate is a little late. Patience is considered a virtue. Allow plenty of time for each appointment.

Don'ts

- Do not be discouraged by belated replies to inquiries, letters and faxes, or by the lack of a reply. Many Armenian firms answer only correspondence that is of vital interest to them. The need to respond promptly is, however, accepted among later generations.

Historical Background

The present-day Republic of Armenia is situated in Southwest Asia, east of Turkey. More precisely, it can be located in the northeast of the Armenian Upland, in Transcaucasia, within the geographical region of the Middle Eastern Crescent. The capital of Armenia is the city of Yerevan, which celebrated its 2,788th anniversary in 2006.

One of the world's oldest civilizations, Armenia is considered by many to be the first country in the world to officially embrace Christianity as its religion around 300 A.D. In the sixth century B.C., the Armenian Empire became one of the most powerful in Asia, stretching from the Caspian Sea to the Mediterranean Sea. Throughout most of its long history, however, Armenia has been invaded by a succession of empires. Under constant threat of domination by foreign forces, Armenians became both cosmopolitan and fierce protectors of their culture and traditions.

Over the centuries, Armenia was conquered by Greeks, Romans, Persians, Byzantines, Mongols, Arabs, Ottoman Turks and Russians. From the 16th century through World War I, major portions of Armenia were controlled by their most brutal invader, the Ottoman Turks. In response to Armenian nationalist stirrings, the Turks massacred thousands of Armenians in 1894 and 1896.

The most horrific massacre took place in April 1915 during World War I, when the Turks ordered the deportation of the Armenian population to the deserts of Syria and Mesopotamia. According to the majority of historians, between 600,000 and 1.5 million Armenians were murdered or died of starvation. The Armenian massacre is considered the first genocide in the 20th century. Turkey denies that genocide took place and claims that a much smaller number died in a civil war.

Armenia was later annexed by the Soviet Army and, in 1922, became part of the U.S.S.R. In 1988, a devastating earthquake killed thousands and wrought economic havoc. Armenia declared its independence from the collapsing Soviet Union on Sept. 23, 1991.

Immigration to the United States

There have been two waves of Armenian immigration to the United States. The first wave began in the middle of the 19th century and ended with U.S. immigration quota laws in 1924. Most of this first wave was from Asia Minor and, directly or indirectly, included survivors of the genocide and deportations by the Ottoman Turks. These initial immigrants were mostly peasants and middle-class tradesmen.

The second wave of immigrants arrived after WWII. This wave of immigration started roughly in the 1950s and gained momentum after 1965 (when immigration quota laws were lifted). These immigrants were more likely to come from the Armenian Diaspora, to have high school and college educations, and to speak English. Emigration from Russia began in the early 20th century. Armenian immigration has been particularly heavy since the country declared independence from the Soviet Union. An estimated 60 percent of the total 8 million Armenians worldwide live outside of the country of Armenia.

The Armenian community can be roughly divided into four major groupings: Armenians from Arab countries, including Lebanon, Syria, Iraq, etc.; Iranian Armenians who had settled in Persia during the 17th century and later during Persian-Turkish-Armenian conflicts; Armenians from the former Soviet Armenia; and third- generation American Armenians who are mostly from Cilicia and Western Armenia.

The vast majority of men and women of Armenian descent in the United States traces their roots to Western Armenia or present-day Turkey, rather than Eastern Armenia.

Religion

Religion has traditionally been an important aspect of Armenian identity. Ethnic identity often coincides with religious affiliation. This might be due to the fact that, by many accounts, Armenia became the first Christian nation in the fourth century A.D. Thus, historically being an Armenian has meant being a Christian. Today, most Armenians belong to one of three religious denominations: Apostolic, Catholic and Protestant.

In 1993, there were 115 Armenian churches in the United States, the majority (81) of which were Apostolic. It is estimated that approximately 65 percent of Armenian Americans are affiliated with the Armenian Apostolic Church, 10 percent are affiliated with the Armenian Protestant Church, and 4 percent are affiliated with the Armenian Catholic Church. The remaining 21 percent do not belong to any Armenian church and some (6 percent) do not identify with any religion. Even among those who are affiliated with a church, church attendance decreases significantly with later generations.

The Armenian American Market

The latest census data (2005) estimate that 57 percent of people reporting Armenian ancestry in the United States are U.S. born, while 43 percent are foreign born.

First and second-generation Armenian immigrants are more likely to be highly active in ethnic churches and formal organizations. Their primary group ties are mostly with fellow Armenians, and they are more likely to marry within the group. Later generations, however, continue to take pride in their Armenian heritage but are more likely to be absent from organized communal life—sporadically attending religious services, cultural performances or social events. While primary group ties are still likely to be with Armenians, they are somewhat more likely to have non-Armenian friends and marry outside the group (often to the disdain of their parents).

Degree of Acculturation

Armenian identity is extremely important, even among those who have grown up in the United States. For example, it is not uncommon for Armenians children to attend Armenian schools, learn the Armenian language and have mostly Armenian friends. Even in the United States, people who are not Armenian are referred to as foreigners among Armenian groups. While later-generation Armenian Americans are less likely to practice the culture of their immigrant parents and grandparents, their identification (sense of "peoplehood" and extreme pride in their Armenian ancestry) does not lessen with time.

Economic Status

More than two-thirds of Armenian professionals and managers are self-employed. At the same time, however, almost half of Armenian males are blue-collar workers, while only approximately one-third are among highly paid white-collar professionals.

In the past, Armenians clustered in the Oriental rug, photoengraving and dry-cleaning businesses. Armenians in New York and Los Angeles have created an occupational niche in the jewelry industry, more specifically as manufacturers of jewelry using precious stones.

Holidays and Celebrations

Traditional U.S. holidays are celebrated among Armenians. Christian holidays, like Good Friday and Easter, are especially important.

New Year—Jan. 1-2: This is the most important holiday of the year, during which people exchange gifts and houses are opened to walk-in guests. There's always an abundance of food on every table, and friends and family go from home to home to visit.

Christmas—Jan. 6: Many Armenians in the United States will celebrate Christmas on Dec. 25. Many Armenians, however, might choose to celebrate the day on Jan. 6, when it is celebrated in Armenia. Christmas is a more solemn occasion and less materialistic than in North American culture. Armenians will attend church on that day and, if possible, take the day off from work. Remembering this day will be appreciated.

Genocide Memorial Day—April 24: April 24, 1915, is the day the Turkish government rounded up and murdered all the Armenian intellectuals in Istanbul. In the United States, the genocide is commemorated by requiems in all Armenian churches, as well as by public gatherings, marches, rallies, speeches and other special events. Many offices might be closed on this day, as it is a solemn occasion.

Independence Day—May 28: May 28, 1918, is the day Armenians claimed their independence from Turkey. During the battle of Sardarabad, Armenian volunteer divisions stopped the Turkish army from advancing farther into Armenian territory. After the battle, Armenian representatives negotiated with the Turks in Tiflis, and the independence of a small portion of the original country was proclaimed. This is an especially joyful day among many Armenians.

Independence Day—Sept. 21: This celebration marks the anniversary of the day in 1991 when Armenians proclaimed independence from the Soviet Union.

NOTES

Asian Indians

Asian Indians
SUMMARY

Demographics

- The Asian Indian community in the United States grew 184 percent from 815,447 in 1990 to 2,319,222 in 2005.

Cultural Insights

- Indians live in a culture that emphasizes the group as opposed to the individual. Thus, an individual's decisions must be in harmony with the family, group and social structures.
- The caste system, a social system based on hierarchy and rigid definition of social class, has played a major role throughout most of India's history. The caste system classifies people by social class, and is based on the notion of reincarnation; if you have led a good and pious life in your previous incarnation, you would reincarnate as a member of a more privileged class.
- As compared to Western communication, traditionally expression is more indirect, as not to offend. Propriety is important; especially the perception of what other people might misconstrue as rude behavior.
- Indians, typically, disapprove of the public display of affection between people of the opposite sex. However, when greeting others they know of the same gender, Indians are known to be warm, friendly and more demonstrative than other Asian populations. As a rule of thumb, when greeting an Indian you do not know well, limit your physical contact to a handshake and avoid hugs or kisses.
- The majority of Indians are Hindu. The traditional Hindu greeting is *namaste*. This greeting is done both verbally and with a gesture of the hands. To perform the *namaste* gesture, hold the palms of your hands together (as if praying) below the chin, nod or bow slightly, and say, "Namaste." This Sanskrit term roughly translates as, "The divinity within me salutes the divinity within you."
- A significant minority of Indians are Muslims. The traditional Muslim greeting is *as-salaam alaikum*, which means, "Peace be unto you," and the usual response is *alaikum salaam*, which means, "Unto you, peace."
- Religious Indian holidays in the United States include Diwali, Eid, Dussehra, Holi, and Christmas. These are the main ones, but people do not take off work for these festivals. Celebrations for them usually take place over the weekend (in the same week of the festival).

Business Practices: Dos and Don'ts

Dos

- Understand that Indians often have a less hurried attitude toward time than North Americans. The concept "time is money" is alien to most Indians. In the United States, however,

Indians have adapted to Western attitudes about time.

- Always present your business card.
- Over time, you can bridge the social distance created by the hierarchical nature of Indian society and its traditions based in the caste system. First, you become acquaintances and, eventually, friends. Then you can do a more effective and successful job of selling or providing a service.
- In India, dinner is eaten late and it is understood that after the meal everyone goes home. If you are planning an interaction where you will host Indian professionals, make sure you make the meal the last thing on the agenda.

Don'ts

- The word "no" has harsh implications in India. Evasive refusals are more common and are considered more polite. Never directly refuse an invitation; just be vague and avoid a time commitment.
- Do not put yourself in situations where a professional will feel lack of deference to or respect for his/her seniority, education and experience. In an attempt to educate a professional on a product or service, one can inadvertently appear to lack humility and to be attempting to show that he/she is smarter than the professional.
- In order to plan an effective event, do not pretend to be an expert on Indian culture. It is OK not to know. Let your clients know of your interest. Research your clients with deference and respect. Do not be afraid to ask questions to learn how to accommodate their needs.
- Pointing with a finger is rude. Indians point with the chin.
- Whistling under any circumstances is considered impolite.
- Never point your feet at a person. Feet are considered unclean.
- When refreshments are offered, it is customary to refuse the first offer but to accept the second or third. It is polite to refuse refreshments at first so as not to put your host through the trouble. However, once the host replies that it is no bother and proceeds to get them for you, it is impolite to refuse, as this might be taken as an insult. Remember to keep this in mind if you offer a refreshment and, at first, you are refused. Don't take the first "no" as the final answer.
- Many Indians consider the head the seat of the soul. Never touch someone else's head, not even to pat the hair of a child.

Asian Indians

Demographics

The growth rate in the Asian Indian American communities between 1990 and 2005 is substantial at 184 percent. The Asian Indian community grew from 815,447 in 1990 to 2,319,222 in 2005.

The 10 most Asian Indian populated states in 2005 were:

1. California (449,722)
2. New York (336,423)
3. New Jersey (228,250)
4. Texas (175,608)
5. Illinois (157,126)

6. Florida (94,043)
7. Georgia (79,169)
8. Michigan (78,466)
9. Virginia (77,208)
10. Pennsylvania (75,159)

The top 10 Asian Indian markets are:

1. New York
2. San Jose, CA
3. Chicago
4. Los Angeles
5. Fremont, CA

6. Houston
7. Edison, NJ
8. Sunnyvale CA
9. Jersey City, NJ
10. Philadelphia

Cultural Insights

Worldview

- Although it had been reduced significantly in comparison to the past, Indians, historically, have had a strong attachment to the caste system. The caste system required many social structures and had many liabilities. The caste system limits individuals to one of four social divisions. Listed in order from the most desirable to the least desirable division they are: Brahman, Kshatriya, Vaisya and Sudra.

- Indians live in a culture that emphasizes the group as opposed to the individual. Thus, an individual's decisions must be in harmony with the family, group and social structures.

Sense of Self

- Indians have a strong preference for the status quo and an aversion to any radical changes. There is a solid understanding of one's role in society. Traditionally, for the masses, there was little anxiety about life because of the acceptance of the status quo and social complacency. Emphasis is on family and the community.

- Indian culture is hierarchical. Age, university degrees, caste and profession determine status.

Sense of Space

- Indians of all ethnic groups disapprove of public displays of affection between people of the opposite sex. Do not touch (except when shaking hands), hug or kiss when greeting.

- However, when greeting others they know of the same gender, Indians are known to be warm, friendly and not as reserved as other Asian populations.

- The majority of Indians are Hindu. Most Hindus avoid public contact between men and women.

- As in Western societies, Indians have a substantial "bubble space"—that is, the comfort zone between people. Hindu Indians tend to stand about 3 to 3-1/2 feet apart.

Communication Style

- As compared to Western communication, expression is more indirect, so as not to offend.

- Maintaining propriety is important, especially because of concerns that others might perceive one's behavior as being rude.

- The traditional Hindu Indian greeting, *namaste,* is done verbally and with a hand gesture. To perform the hand gesture that accompanies the *namaste* greeting, hold the palms of your hands together (as if praying) below the chin, nod or bow slightly, and say, "Namaste" (roughly translated in Sanskirt, this means "The divinity in me salutes the divinity in you").

- A significant number of Indians are Muslims. The traditional Muslim greeting is *asalaam alaikum*, which means,"Peace be unto you," and the usual response is *alaikum salaam*, which means, "Unto you, peace."

- Among Indians, a side-to-side toss of one's head indicates agreement, although Westerners might interpret it as meaning "no". Watch carefully: The Indian head toss is not quite the same as the Western negative nod. The Western "no" is done with the face looking from side-to-side. The Indian side-to-side toss is similar to having the ears subtly bounce from each shoulder.

- Titles are highly valued by Indians. Always use professional titles, such as "professor", and "doctor". Do not address someone by his/her first name unless you are asked to do so, or are close friends.

Eye Contact

- Eye contact is important in order to convey sincerity and attentiveness to the speaker.

Language

- Hindi is the national language in India. English has also been retained as a language for official communication. There are 15 major languages and 844 dialects that are spoken throughout the country.

- Indians in America do not experience the same level of difficulty in language immersion as other immigrants because of English colonization of India and their exposure to the English language.

Time and Time Consciousness

- Indians are not known for being punctual socially. In fact, it is customary to arrive a little late to meetings. There is an appreciation for flexibility. Assimilation to Western operating procedures, however, has modified this behavior among Indian professionals and businesspeople in the United States.

Values and Norms

- Indians have strong religious beliefs.

- There is a rigid structure of inequality. The caste system has ingrained Indians with the belief that there are tangible, qualitative differences between the classes.

- Male chauvinism is strong. In India, women traditionally have had few privileges. Among the educated in India and among Indian women in the United States, this has changed. Gender roles, however, are clearly defined among most people.

Business Practices: Dos and Don'ts

Dos

- Understand that Indians often have a less hurried attitude toward time than North Americans. The concept "time is money" is alien to most Indians. In the United States, however, Indians have adapted to the majority's business norms.

- Always present your business card.

- You can bridge the social distance created by the hierarchical nature of Indian society via a relationship that develops over time. Initially, you become acquaintances and, eventually, friends. Then you can do a more effective and successful job of selling or providing a service.

- In India, dinner is eaten late and it is understood that after the meal, everyone goes home. If you are planning an interaction where you will host Indian professionals, make sure you make the meal the last thing on the agenda.

Don'ts

- The word "no" has harsh implications in India. Evasive refusals are more common and are considered more polite. Never directly refuse an invitation; just be vague and avoid a time commitment.

- Do not put yourself in situations where a professional will feel lack of deference to or respect for his/her seniority, education and experience. In an attempt to educate a professional on a product or service, one can inadvertently appear to lack humility and to attempt to show that he/she is smarter than the professional.

- Conventional Western "wining and dining" might not be effective with Indian professionals. The less acculturated, typically, do not bring their wives to American restaurants. Depending on their level of acculturation, wives might dress in traditional Indian fashion (in saris) and they might be uncomfortable at events where they do not feel they would fit in. If other Indian women who are their peers attend, chances are they will too. Additionally, again depending on their level of acculturation, they might prefer Indian food as opposed to American food.

- In order to plan an effective event, do not pretend to be an expert on Indian culture. It is OK not to know. Let your clients know of your interest. Research their culture with deference and respect. Do not be afraid to ask the questions necessary to learn how to accommodate and best serve these clients.

- Pointing with a finger is rude. Indians point with the chin.

- Whistling under any circumstances is considered impolite.

- Never point your feet at a person. Feet are considered unclean.

- When refreshments are offered, it is customary to refuse the first offer but to accept the second or third. It is polite to refuse refreshments at first so as not to put your host through the trouble. However, once the host replies that it is no bother at all and proceeds to get them for you, it is impolite to refuse, and this might be taken as an insult. Remember to keep this in mind if you offer refreshments and, at first, you are refused. Don't take the first "no" as the final answer.

- Many Indians consider the head the seat of the soul. Never touch someone else's head, not even to pat the hair of a child.

Historical Background

Beginning around 3000 B.C., a population that was to become Indian flourished in the fertile valley of the Indus River. As they made the transition from nomads to settled agriculturists, the early Indians developed village communities. Hinduism, at that time, was at a nascent stage, and Sanskrit, from which most North Indian scripts are derived, was the prevailing language.

In the third century B.C., the north was consolidated into one great empire under Chandragupta Maurya. His grandson, Ashoka the Great (268-231 B.C.), however, is better known. Deeply affected by observing a bloodbath on the battlefield, he chose to practice and preach the Buddhist philosophy of nonviolence, both in India and abroad. During this period in the south, maritime trade with Rome flourished.

Between A.D. 320 and 480, often referred to as the Golden Age of the Guptas, India saw the flowering of art, culture, literature and science. Erudite treatises on subjects ranging from medicine and mathematics to astronomy and even lovemaking (such as the famed *Kamasutra*) were written.

In the 13th century, Qutub-ud-din Aibak established Muslim rule in India. In the 16th century, Babur established Mughal rule. His grandson, Akbar (1562-1605) is even now viewed as a progressive ruler, for he sought in many ways—through administrative systems, art, culture and even religion—to unify different cultures. Physically, too, the splintering kingdom became an empire. Another ruler, Shahjehan—famed for his immortal creation, the Taj Mahal—took Mughal glory to its zenith. Aurangzeb was the last great emperor of the Mughal dynasty. The 17th century brought the Europeans, with the British, French, Dutch and Portuguese setting up trading posts. The Battle of Plassey in 1757 was decisive, with the British gaining supremacy over the other colonial powers.

British rule provided India with a railroad network, a bureaucracy, and a common language— English. However, national aspirations and the desire for self-determination on the part of the Indians resulted in the First War of Independence in 1857. Though brutally suppressed, the uprising marked the beginning of a struggle in which the Indian National Congress, founded in 1885, formed the backbone.

India's most important contemporary historical figure emerged during this period of struggle: Mohandas K. Gandhi. Gandhi legitimized the practice of nonviolence for political and social change in India and the rest of the world.

Independence from Great Britain came in 1947. To Gandhi's despair, however, the country was partitioned into Hindu India and Muslim Pakistan. The last two months of his life were spent trying to end the appalling violence that ensued. To accomplish this task, he fasted to the brink of death, an act that finally quelled the riots. In January, 1948, at the age of 79, Gandhi was killed by an assassin as he walked through a crowded garden in New Delhi to take evening prayers.

Today, hostilities between mostly Muslim Pakistan and mostly Hindu India continue to escalate over a disputed region in northeast India called Kashmir. Kashmir is mostly Muslim, and Pakistanis contend that the region should be theirs. Skirmishes occur on a regular basis along the borders of Kashmir, causing regional instability and heightened tension between the two nuclear powers.

Immigration to the United States

In the late 1800s, a number of Indians immigrated into the northwestern United States and Canada. A large number of them worked in laying the railroads in the western United States. As with many other immigrant populations, the main reason for their stay in America was to save money to send home to their families.

During the early part of the 20th century, U.S. immigration policy was geared toward the exclusion of non-European immigrants, primarily Asians. Indians then living in America experienced tremendous hardship. Numerous states, including California, passed a series of laws designed to undermine the legality of their residential status.

Toward the end of World War II, President Theodore Roosevelt started to lift immigration restrictions on Asians. The Chinese Exclusion Act was repealed, and so was the Indian Regional Exclusion Act.

Indian immigration picked up considerably in the late 1960s and early 1970s. These immigrants included a number of Indian doctors, who came to fill the shortage of physicians created by the Vietnam War. The momentum gained during this time led to an increase in Indian immigration through the 1980s and 1990s.

Just like other immigrants, Indians move to the United States for financial and professional opportunities. The average per capita income is much higher in the United States than in India. Professionals can earn even more in the United States and have a much greater opportunity for advancement.

Currently, there has been a great demand for highly skilled Indian professionals, especially in the software and advanced technology fields. This has led to a high demand for H1B Visas (special work permit visas) for these workers, especially those in high-tech firms located in California's Silicon Valley in and around San Jose. This is a logical explanation for the growth of the Indian population in northern California. These highly trained and sought after professionals reflect the high quality of education that they received in India.

Religion

Religion plays a major role in the daily lives of most Indians. Two of the world's great religions—Buddhism and Hinduism—were born in India. Although 83 percent of the people are Hindu, India also has one of the world's largest Muslim populations. Other major religions include Christianity, Sikhism and Jainism. This religious composition is similar for Indians in the United States.

The goal of Hinduism is freedom (of the soul, or Atman) from endless reincarnation and the suffering inherent in existence and resulting from bad karma. Karma comprises the actions the individual commits while in this present life and also an accumulation of actions from past lives.

The caste system is part of Hinduism. Caste divides society into four social classes. The highest class is called the priest class, or the Brahmans. The lowest class is referred to as the laborer class, or Sudras. One inherits class at birth, based on one's karma, or tally of good and bad deeds from previous lives.

Muslims practice Islam, one of the world's largest monotheistic faiths. Islam originated in Saudi Arabia and was founded by the Prophet Muhammad. Islam is based on the teachings of the Koran, the holy Muslim book of teachings. (Note: For a more detailed description of the Muslim religion and its practices, please see the section on Muslim Americans)

Guru Nanak founded Sikhism in India in the 15th century in an attempt to reconcile Hindu and Islamic religions. His followers were called Sikhs, or "seekers of truth." The fundamental belief of Sikhism is that there is one God and many paths to reach him. The name of God is Truth, or "Sat Nam." At the heart of Sikh worship is the Holy Scripture, called the Guru Granth

Sahib. Any place where the Guru Granth Sahib is placed and treated respectfully can be called Gurdwara, which is a Sikh place of worship. The main principles of Sikhism are belief in one God, belief in the 10 spiritual masters (gurus) and their teachings, acceptance of the Sikh holy book as a living guru, rejection of the caste system, belief in the equality of men and women, belief in reincarnation, and the belief that salvation is attained through meditation and service.

Guru Gobind Singh, the 10th guru and the last in human form, created the Khalsa, a spiritual brotherhood and sisterhood of initiated Sikhs. Khalsa must wear five items at all times, called the "5 Ks": Kesh, or uncut hair and beard, which are gifts from God, and a turban or scarf; Kangha, a wooden comb representing cleanliness; Katchera, a type of cotton underwear to remind one of their commitment to purity; Kara, a steel bracelet symbolizing a link to God; and Kirpan, a short sword that is a symbol of commitment to truth and justice.

Besides not cutting their hair, Khalsa do not consume tobacco products, alcohol or illicit drugs, and they avoid meat not humanely slaughtered. Kosher and Halal meats are forbidden for Sikhs. They do not eat any ritual meat prepared by either sacrificing the animal to please God or by killing the animal slowly to drain out the blood.

Since Sept. 11, 2001, many Indians who practice Hinduism and Sikhism have been the targets of hate crimes by people who mistakenly believe they are Muslims.

Language

Hindi is the national language. English has also been retained as a language for official communication. There are 15 major languages and 844 dialects that are spoken throughout India.

The Asian Indian Market

Asian Indians were the second largest Asian group (2,319,222) in the United States behind the Chinese (2,882,257) in 2005. According to the 2005 Census Community Survey, Indian American median family income was $73,575 as compared to the national median family income of $46,242. The high income clearly reflects the advanced educational levels achieved by the community. Their per capita income is the highest among any ethnic group in the United States. The estimated annual buying power of Indian Americans in the United States is around $20 billion.

Degree of Acculturation

Unlike many other Asian immigrants, Asian Indians have had an easier time acculturating in the United States because of British influence over Indian culture. Asian Indians in America are usually fluent in English and are familiar with Western ways.

Economic Status

Most Indians currently immigrating to the United States are either professionals or the family members of Asian Indians who are already U.S. citizens. The Indian community in the United States is currently the most well educated and prosperous one. According to the Census American Community Survey in 2005, 90.4 percent of Indians in the U.S. had completed high school, 68.2 percent had completed college and a stunning 36 percent had completed master's or doctoral degrees. Their education and income levels are higher than other Asian American groups, Whites, Hispanics and Blacks.

More than 5,000 Indian Americans today serve as faculty members in institutions of higher education in the United States. About 300,000 Indian Americans work in technology firms in California's Silicon Valley. They account for more than 15 percent of high-tech startups in that region. The median income of Indian Americans in that region is estimated to be $125,000 a year.

Holidays and Celebrations

Most festivals in India are determined by the solar-lunar calendar. Some dates vary each year, while others remain the same

Maghi (Sikh): *Maghi* is a commemoration of the Forty Immortals, (40 followers of Guru Gobindh Singh) who fought against the Mughal army and were martyred. On this day, Sikhs will visit gurdwaras (temples) and listen to kirtan (the musical recitation of hymns from the Sri Guru Granth Sahib, or Holy Scripture). It is usually celebrated in January.

Holi (Hindu): During this holiday celebrating the advent of spring, men, women and children revel in throwing colored powder and water on their friends. This is the most boisterous of all Hindu festivals, observed all over northern and central India. It heralds the end of winter. Greetings and sweets are exchanged.

Holla Mohalla (Sikh): Holla Mohalla is the Sikh celebration of spring. Traditionally, *Holla Mohalla* is an annual festival celebrated in Punjab on the day following the festival of *Holi*. Sikhs will gather and perform military exercises and mock battles, followed by music, poetry, religious lectures and a parade. This holiday is generally celebrated in March.

Vaisakhi (Sikh): This holiday commemorates the beginning of the solar year. For Sikhs, it also recognizes the creation of the Khalsa (the Sikh brotherhood) and rejection of the Indian caste system. On this day, Sikhs visit gurdwaras (temples) and might have parades and fairs.

Mawlid al Nabi (Muslim): Prophet Muhammad's birthday. This day is celebrated with varying degrees of enthusiasm throughout the Muslim world. It generally falls in spring.

Dussehra (Hindu): This festival celebrates the end of the summer and the beginning of cooler weather. For Hindus, this occasion marks the triumph of Lord Ram over Ravana; the victory of good over evil, and is celebrated with lots of food and merriment over a 10-day period.

Diwali (Hindu, Sikh): *Diwali* is the Indian festival of lights, and both Hindus and Sikhs celebrate it. This festival of lights takes place over a course of a week and symbolizes the vanquishing of dark forces and the immersion of light, or positive energy. Elaborate candlelight processions take place during these celebrations. Sikhs often light lamps outside of gurdwaras (temples) and distribute sweets.

Ramadan (Muslim): *Ramadan* is the ninth month of the Islamic year and is known as the month of fasting. During *Ramadan*, especially for observant Muslims, there is no eating, drinking or sexual activity between dawn and sunset (people physically unable to fast, such as the sick or those on a difficult journey, are excluded). During the night, Muslims eat, drink (alcohol is forbidden) and carry on normally. If possible, some Muslims take time off from their work for the last 10 days of *Ramadan* in order to isolate themselves from worldly affairs.

Eid-al-Fitr (Muslim): Celebrates the end of Ramadan, the Muslim month of fasting. It is an occasion of feasting and rejoicing. The faithful gather in mosques to pray; friends and relatives meet to exchange greetings.

Christmas—Dec. 25: Christian Indians celebrate Christmas.

Gurupurbs (Sikh): *Gurupurbs* are anniversaries throughout the year associated with the lives of gurus. These days are often celebrated by a cover to cover reading of the Sri Guru Granth Sahib (Akand Path), a musical recitation of hymns from the Sri Guru Granth Sahib (*kirtan*) and lectures on Sikhism (*katha*). Some gurdwaras offer free sweets to the public. Some of the larger Gurupurbs are:

> Birthday of Guru Gobindh Singh Sahib
> Martyrdom of Guru Arjan Dev Sahib
> Installation of Holy Scripture as Guru Granth Sahib
> Birthday of Guru Nanak Dev Sahib
> Martyrdom of Guru Tegh Bahadur Sahib

NOTES

Central Americans

Central Americans
SUMMARY

Demographics

- According to census updates made in the year 2005, there are approximately 3.1 million Central Americans in the United States. However, some demographers believe the actual number is around 6 million.
- Salvadorans and Guatemalans are the largest groups of Central Americans in the country.

Cultural Insights

- Kinship ties are generally quite strong and are the core of the Central American social structure.
- Central Americans might appear to have an informal, relaxed way of conducting business.
- Although the emotional impact of an interaction can be more important, the objective information and facts are still essential. This is particularly important in the context of sales, where developing a relationship based on an emotional connection can make the difference between success and failure.
- Business decisions will often favor friends and family over expertise.
- Traditionally, lunch is the main meal of the day. However, in the United States, this is changing.
- Business might take place at a much slower pace.
- Formality is the norm. Maintain a formal stance until your associate indicates that informal contact is appropriate.
- Central American groups, especially Salvadorans and Guatemalans, are among the most undocumented of national-origin groups in the United States.
- Most Central Americans in the United States celebrate traditional U.S. holidays, as well as some that are common to Mexican Americans.

Business Practices: Dos and Don'ts

Dos

- Although Central Americans can be somewhat relaxed about punctuality, it is important that you arrive on time. It is OK to be a little late for social occasions.
- Try to schedule appointments as far in advance as possible.
- Spend time forming a friendship before jumping into business discussions.
- If you notice that your client is not proficient in English and if you speak Spanish, politely ask them if they would prefer to speak in Spanish or English This can improve rapport and lead to a closer relationship. It is definitely to your advantage.

Don'ts

- Be careful not to refer to people from Central American countries as Mexican.

- Avoid frank criticism or any behavior that would demean another person in public.
- Don't be surprised if you receive a limp handshake. Adjust your grip to that of your associate.
- Avoid gifts of white flowers. They are reserved for funerals.

Central Americans
SUMMARY

Demographics

According to census updates in the year 2005, there are approximately 3,084,580 Central Americans in the United States. However, some demographers feel that the number is closer to 6 million. This difference relates to the fact that a vast number of Salvadoran and Guatemalan populations are undocumented (approximately 40 percent), as well as to the belief that many of the Central Americans who did participate in the Census did not accurately specify their ethnicity. They comprise 7 percent of the total Hispanic population (41,870,703) in 2005. Salvadorans and Guatemalans are the biggest groups of Central Americans in the country. There are 1,239,640 Salvadorans (2.9 percent of the total Hispanic population) and 758,898 Guatemalans (1.8 percent of the Hispanic population) in the United States.

The 10 most Central American populated states in 2005 were (NA indicates that exact population figures are not available):

1. California (1,000,547)
2. Texas (341,330)
3. New York (380,940)
4. Florida (238,273)
5. New Jersey (132,547)
6. Maryland (122,178)
7. Virginia (NA)
8. Illinois (NA)
9. Massachusetts (NA)
10. Georgia (NA)

Cultural Insights

Worldview

- The Central American worldview is based on respect for past struggles and desire for political, social and economic freedom.

- Kinship ties are generally quite strong and are the core of the Central American social structure.

- Although Central Americans might appear to have an informal, relaxed way of conducting business, formality, at least initially, is called for.

Sense of Self

- Self-identity is largely centered on one's place in the family, his/her position in the social system and his/her performance in the group.

Sense of Space

- Central Americans usually converse at closer distances than North Americans.

- There is a good deal more physical contact (e.g., touching of the arm, shoulder and lapel) among Central Americans than among some other cultures.

Communication Style

- Close male friends might hug or pat each other on the back in greeting. Close female friends might hug or kiss each other on the cheek.

- The Spanish language provides forms of formal and nonformal address (different use of *usted* vs. *tu* for the pronoun you, polite and familiar commands, and the use of titles of respect before people's first names, such as *Don* or *Doña*). In nonformal settings, conversations between Spanish speakers are usually loud and fast when compared to similar English-language conversations in the United States.

Eye Contact

- Maintaining eye contact is important. Looking away might project distrustfulness. However, if you are dealing with someone who is younger or from a rural environment, he/she might not maintain eye contact. For these individuals, this behavior is a demonstration of respect for you.

- Unacculturated Latinos also might avert their eyes in unpleasant or highly charged situations and confrontations.

Language

- Spanish is the official language of the majority of the countries in Central America. The exception is Belize, where the official language is English.

- Because of the high density of people of Latino origin in border states and in major metropolitan areas where Central Americans often live, the Spanish language is basically maintained. Spanish-English bilingualism is prevalent among later generations of immigrants, but the majority of immigrants are recent arrivals who primarily speak Spanish and might have some difficulty with English. However, those in professional positions and with more education will most likely speak English fluently.

Time and Time Consciousness

- While North Americans are usually expected to be on time, punctuality is not a high priority for most Central Americans. It is important to arrive on time for business appointments, but it is OK to be a little late for social occasions.

Values and Norms

- Humanitarian values are strong among Central Americans.

- *Familismo* has to do with the high degree of interpersonal bonding within the Central American family, resulting in greater identification with the group and dependence on the family. Recent studies also have demonstrated the importance of the nuclear and extended family as a source of social support. Latinos might "adopt" close friends as *compadres* and family members in the absence of blood ties. Family and family life are extremely important, and decisions are usually made with the best interest of the family or larger group in mind. Business decisions will often favor friends and family over expertise.

- *Machismo* characterizes the male gender role in Latino society. It stresses virility, independence and physical strength. It supports the idea that women are subordinate and inferior to men. However, with more exposure to North American attitudes, this belief is being questioned.

- *Marianismo* has been characterized as the complement of *machismo*. *Marianismo* defines the role of the ideal woman, modeled after the Virgin Mary, as based on chastity, renunciation and sacredness, while reinforcing obedience.

- There is a strong work ethic among Central Americans, as well as a strong belief in mutual aid—especially within the immediate family.

- The emotional impact of an interaction can be more important than the objective information and facts. This is particularly important in the context of sales, where developing a relationship based on an emotional connection can mean the difference between success and failure.

Business Practices: Dos and Don'ts

Dos

- Although Central Americans can be more relaxed about punctuality, it is important that you arrive on time. It is OK to be a little late for social occasions.

- Try to schedule appointments as far in advance as possible.

- Be patient. Business might take place at a much slower pace.

- Personal relationships are generally quite important in business dealings. Spend time forming a friendship before jumping into business discussions.

- Formality is the norm. Remain formal in your interactions until your associate indicates that informality is appropriate.

- If you notice that your client is not proficient in English and you speak Spanish, politely ask whether his/her preference would be to speak in Spanish or English. This can improve rapport and lead to a closer relationship. It is definitely to your advantage.

Don'ts

- A common misperception is that all Latinos are Mexican. Be careful not to refer to people from Central American countries as Mexican.

- Personal honor is important for Central Americans. Avoid frank criticism or any behavior that would demean another person in public.

- Don't be surprised if you receive a limp handshake. Adjust your grip to that of your associate. Also, handshakes might last longer than is normal among mainstream Americans.

- Avoid gifts of white flowers. They are reserved for funerals.

Historical Background

Central America includes the countries of Guatemala, Belize, El Salvador, Honduras, Nicaragua, Costa Rica and Panama.

Originally, Central America—the area between Mexico and Colombia—was home to a large pre-Columbian population, the most important of whom were the Maya. At the time of the "discovery" of Central America by Christopher Columbus in 1502 and the subsequent arrival of Europeans to the area, Central America contained a population of approximately 6 million indigenous inhabitants. Battles with European conquerors and disease decimated the indigenous populations. The Spanish enslaved or reduced to serfdom those who remained, establishing an agricultural society based on institutions they had brought from Spain. Their numbers decreased dramatically so that by the year 1600, no more than 1 million Central American Indians remained. Even with the general population explosion of the last 50 years, the indigenous population only accounts for about 4 million to 5 million of Central America's 29 million people. The largest portion of Central America's contemporary population is *mestizo*, or of mixed indigenous and European descent.

Soon after the conquest, a rigid class- and color-based society developed, with the darker-skinned natives at the bottom, *mestizos* (those of mixed indigenous and European descent) made up the working class, and the *criollos* (those of European descent born in the New World) and the *peninsulars* (those from Spain) made up the elite.

Allegiance to Spain was severed via rebellion in 1821, after which the region became part of the Mexican Empire. The United Province of Central America was formed in 1823. After years of political and economic struggle, Guatemala, Honduras, El Salvador, Nicaragua and Costa Rica emerged as independent republics. Yet by this time, England—with its influence in Belize and along the Caribbean coast—emerged as the dominant external force of the region. Since the end of the 19th century, the United States has been the dominant external force in Central America. For example, the United Fruit Company was a major force in Central America's economy in the early 20th century. This U.S. company was known as the "Octopus" among Central Americans because the U.S. was reaping the reward from the region's natural resources.

The second half of the 20th century has seen persistent poverty, political instability and social injustice in many of the Central American republics still undergoing modernization. One of the most significant problems confronting all Central American countries is the difficulty of bringing about considerable socioeconomic development without affecting the democratic rights of their populations.

Immigration to the United States

Emigration from Central America increased significantly because of civil strife and the liberalization of immigration policy in the United States after 1965. In the 1970s, the Panamanians and Hondurans constituted the largest Central American groups in the United States. However, the majority of Central Americans arrived more recently when, in the 1980s, populations from El Salvador and Guatemala grew dramatically because of war and civil strife in those countries. Central American immigrants flocked to the Northeast, Pacific Coast and Gulf Coast states, and the flow of undocumented immigrants from the region—especially from El Salvador and Nicaragua—was substantial.

Many Central American immigrants were women in service or low-paying white-collar jobs. These immigrants also found work as a result of the high demand for household, childcare and elder-care workers, as well as maintenance service in office buildings, hotels and hospitals.

Religion

Although traditional reference sources state that 90 to 95 percent of Central Americans are Roman Catholic, there has been a great deal of conversion to Evangelical Protestant denominations in the past several years. For example, one recent study estimates that 25 percent of the Guatemalan population is Protestant. Although at present there is a lack of accurate data, we believe that this trend toward a growth in Protestantism is reflected among Central Americans in the United States.

The Central American Market

Central American groups, especially Salvadorans and Guatemalans, have tended to have less income and work in informal sectors of the economy. As with Mexicans, ties to home countries are strong, and a large portion of earned income is sent back to their home countries in the form of remittances. Recent estimates suggest that U.S. remittances to Latin America run in the billions. Often remittances sent to Latin America are greater than U.S. foreign aid to those regions. While this is a major source of income for their home economies, at the same time it can limit their economic progress here.

Degree of Acculturation

There is not much to speak of in terms of generational differences when it comes to these groups, because their population in the United States. is a relatively new one. The second, native-born generation is relatively young. Only 3 percent of working-age Guatemalans were U.S.-born in 1990. However, preliminary data does show increased levels of education among immigrants who came here as young children. In terms of acculturation, these groups are integrating into the Latino/Mexican American mainstream in areas such as Southern California.

Economic Status

Salvadorans and Guatemalans tend to have lower educational levels than other Central Americans, and they have low median incomes compared to non-Central Americans. Salvadorans and Guatemalans are as likely as their Mexican counterparts to be engaged in service occupations and as household workers. They have developed occupational niches as textile workers, janitors, cooks and painters.

Salvadorans and Guatemalans born in the United States make approximately two-thirds of what Whites make. More recent immigrants earn less. The numbers for other Central American groups are slightly higher.

Central American men have higher-than-average labor-force participation rates. This is most likely because of the immigrant work ethic.

Holidays and Celebrations

Although Central America is composed of several countries, the majority of Central Americans in the United States are from Guatemala and El Salvador. Most Central Americans in the United States celebrate traditional U.S. holidays, as well as those common to Mexicans. Christian holidays, like Christmas and Easter, are especially important.

Año Nuevo (New Year's Day)—Jan. 1: Traditional Western holiday.

Day of the Magi/Day of the Three Kings (*Día de los Santos Reyes/Magos*)—Jan. 6: Traditionally, it is this day when gifts are dispensed (as opposed to Christmas Day) to commemorate the day when the Magi (The Three Kings) presented gifts to Jesus of Nazareth. This day is celebrated differently among different Latino groups in the United States and is losing some of its significance with the increased focus on Christmas. It is mostly considered a day for the children to receive gifts and celebrate.

Easter and *La Semana Santa* (Holy Week): Easter is one of the most important holy days of the year for Latino Catholics. It is celebrated nearly everywhere in Latin America and Spain with religious observances and various types of processions. *Semana Santa* begins with Palm Sunday (*el Domingo de Ramos*), includes Good Friday (*el Viernes Santo*) and ends with Easter (*la Pascua de Resurrección*). The week is meant to mark the triumphant entry of Jesus into Jerusalem, followed by his death and resurrection.

Independence Day—Sept. 15: This day marks Independence Day for El Salvador, Costa Rica, Guatemala, Honduras and Nicaragua. Cities with a large Central American presence will often celebrate with a parade.

Hispanic Heritage Month—Sept. 15-Oct. 15: A month designated by the U.S. government to celebrate and explore Latino history and influence in this country.

Day of the Dead (*Día de los Muertos*)—Nov. 1: Celebrated in Mexico and in certain parts of the United States and Central America. Traditionally, it is a day to celebrate and honor one's ancestors. Celebrations can vary from setting up altars in homes for deceased family members to attending a family dinner in honor of one's ancestors. This celebration originated during pre-Hispanic times. Although the ritual has since been merged with Catholic theology, it still maintains the basic principles of the Aztec ritual, such as the presentation of candy skulls.

Las Posadas—Dec. 16-24: Celebrates Joseph's and Mary's search for shelter in Bethlehem with candlelight processions that end at nativity scenes. Las Posadas continues through Dec. 24.

Christmas Eve (*Nochebuena*) and Christmas (*Navidad*)—Dec. 24-25: With the rest of the Christian world, Central Americans celebrate Christmas day. Christmas Eve (Dec. 24) is widely observed, and dinner and festivities take place on this day rather than on the traditional U.S. celebration day, Dec. 25.

Quinceañeras: A *quinceañera*, or 15th-birthday celebration, is a rite of passage for young Catholic Hispanic girls, and is growing in popularity in the United States. The roots of the ceremony are found in a combination of indigenous and Spanish customs, and it is meant to represent a girl's emergence into womanhood. Girls are required to attend a year of religion classes before the celebration, which usually begins with a Mass, and then followed by a party. The celebration itself tends be quite extravagant, and can rival a wedding in nature. The girl will wear an elaborate dress that symbolizes femininity, a gold medallion that expresses her faith, a ring that represents her spiritual and communal responsibilities, and a crown that symbolizes her living a Christian life. She will have 14 maids of honor, or *damas* (one for each year of childhood), and each will have a male escort—all of whom will perform a symbolic dance for the occasion. These events can cost thousands of dollars, and friends and relatives will often help with expenses.

NOTES

Chinese Americans

Chinese Americans

SUMMARY

Demographics

- Chinese Americans comprise the largest Asian subgroup in the United States, with the population growing 75 percent from 1.6 million in 1990 to nearly 2.9 million in 2005.
- The most Chinese populated state is California, followed by New York.

Cultural Insights

- The Chinese are highly influenced by the opinions and norms of the group.
- Traditional Chinese families focus on filial piety. This means that older adults are viewed with great respect. Chinese children are taught that their behavior reflects highly on the family.
- Chinese Americans value discretion, restraint of strong emotions, and not embarrassing others or losing face themselves.
- Frugality is important for the Chinese. They are price-conscious.
- The most important holidays are the Chinese New Year (Lunar New Year, celebrated sometime between late January to early February) and Zhong Qiu Jie (Mid-Autumn Festival).

Business Practices: Dos and Don'ts

Dos

- It is important to remember that a Chinese person might have grown up in or had significant life experiences in many places around the globe.
- When in doubt, dress conservatively.
- Appointments should be made as far in advance as possible.
- In pricing and numbering, use the numbers 8 and 6. In Chinese the number 8 sounds like "becoming wealthy", and 6 sounds like "happiness".
- Age is respected by the Chinese. If your client is 50 or older, he/she will command respect.
- Always follow through with your promises.
- Spend a little time on small talk about family, especially about children and their education.
- Always prepare many alternatives in order to give the Chinese negotiator room to negotiate several options with dignity.

Don'ts

- Don't mistake different Asian ancestries.
- Don't assume the individual speaks Chinese or prefers to speak Chinese.
- Don't butcher names over and over again.
- Because the Chinese believe humility is a virtue, never exaggerate your ability to deliver.

- Don't show off.
- Don't use a Chinese person's first name unless you know him/her well.
- The Chinese do not like to be touched by people they do not know. This is especially important to remember when dealing with older people, people in important positions, and females.

Chinese Americans

Demographics

Chinese Americans comprise the largest Asian subgroup in the United States, with the population growing 75 percent from 1.6 million in 1990 to nearly 2.9 million in 2005.

The 10 most Chinese populated states in 2005 were:

1. California (1,113,844)
2. New York (504,041)
3. Texas (137,544)
4. New Jersey (122,931)
5. Massachusetts (103,748)
6. Illinois (90,569)
7. Washington (72,135)
8. Pennsylvania (65,042)
9. Maryland (59,933)
10. Florida (55,508)

The top five Chinese markets in the United States were:

1. New York (471,681) *
2. Los Angeles (463,970) *
3. San Francisco (208,386) *
4. Boston (100,789) *
5. Chicago (82,406) *

Includes surrounding cities

Cultural Insights

Worldview

- The Chinese are highly influenced by the opinions and norms of the group.

- Chinese culture values hierarchy and formality. However, remember that traditional Chinese culture is formal. You should take the lead from your client as to how formal to be. Your client's level of formality might change depending on the setting. Thus, for example, he/she might be more formal at work and less formal in social settings.

- Chinese Americans put heavy emphasis on personal duty.

Sense of Self

- Chinese culture puts emphasis on harmony and long-term achievements.

- The Chinese value the past.

Sense of Space

- The huge population in China has resulted in the need for less personal space.

Communication Style

- Traditionally, the Chinese have preferred indirect communication. They might not like to be asked or be forced to answer too directly.

- They value discretion, restraint of strong emotions and not embarrassing others or losing face themselves.

- In negotiations, they tend to wait for the other party to declare their position.

Eye Contact

- Avoid direct eye contact, particularly with unacculturated Chinese women.

Language

- The Chinese American population is further defined by its two major language dialects: Mandarin and Cantonese. The speech varieties spoken in Beijing (Mandarin) and Guang Zhou (Cantonese) are not mutually intelligible and are actually different languages. Yet traditionally and according to their speakers, they are dialects. This perception is partly due to the fact that speakers of Cantonese and Mandarin (and speakers of other Chinese languages) use the same writing system.

    Mandarin is the official language of China and Taiwan, spoken by the Chinese in Northern China and Taiwan.
    Cantonese was traditionally—and continues to be—spoken by many of the Chinese in Canton (Guang Zhou) Province and Hong Kong. However, please note that younger Chinese throughout China and Hong Kong also learn and speak Mandarin.

- After Mao Tse-tung took control of China in 1949, he decreed that Mandarin would be the official spoken language of China. He also introduced a system to simplify the complex written Chinese language.

- The major Chinese print media in the United States, with their dramatically high daily readership levels, are published in traditional characters. In the academic community, simplified Chinese characters might be used without bias. However, in today's business world, the use of traditional Chinese characters is the norm.

- 83.2 percent of Chinese Americans speak Chinese at home.

- 46 percent admit to not speaking English well.

- Bilingual written materials are preferred. Not only will they indicate your commitment to the

Chinese market, but they also indicate an acknowledgment that first-generation Chinese might feel more comfortable reading in their own language. Use traditional Chinese characters as opposed to simplified characters. Because of its connection with Mao Tse-tung and the Communist Party, simplified Chinese might be considered offensive to some Taiwanese nationals and those who grew up in Hong Kong before the Chinese government reclaimed it from the British. Furthermore, those who read and write simplified Chinese will be able to understand traditional Chinese, while the reverse is not always true.

- More acculturated bilinguals do not trust materials that are only presented in Chinese. Their main concern is the accuracy of the information after the translation.

Time and Time Consciousness

- In business dealings, Chinese do try to be on time, but socially they might be more relaxed about time.

- In Chinese tradition, no one is exempt from apologizing. Be sure to apologize sincerely if you are late, even if it was not your fault.

Values and Norms

- Chinese culture is contextual. Thus, it is not only what you say to a client that matters, but also how they feel they are treated.

- Frugality is important to the Chinese. They are price-conscious.

- Chinese Americans plan for the long term and emphasize education for success.

- Traditional Chinese families focus on filial piety. This means that older adults are treated with great respect. Chinese children are taught that their behavior highly reflects on the family.

Business Practices: Dos and Don'ts

Dos

- It is important to remember that a Chinese person might have grown up in or had significant life experiences in many places around the globe. Chinese from mainland China, Hong Kong and Taiwan have many unifying cultural traits, but there are some differences in their experiences and reactions to situations.

- When in doubt, dress conservatively. You'll have more credibility at the onset, especially if you are young.

- Appointments should be made as far in advance as possible.

- Provide perks when possible. Chinese people are known to like deals and extras.

- In pricing and numbering, use the numbers 8 and 6. In Chinese the number 8 sounds like "becoming wealthy", and 6 sounds like "happiness".

- Wrap gifts in the following colors:

  Red—symbolizes luck.
  Pink and yellow—symbolize happiness and prosperity.

- Age is respected by the Chinese. If your client is 50 or older, he or she will command respect.

- Always follow through with your promises. Whenever possible, deliver more than what you promised.

- Refer to other (local) Chinese you have worked with. It shows that you have credibility.

- Spend a little time with small talk about family, especially about children and, if appropriate, their education. It is good to shows your interest, but do not chat so long as to interfere with business.

- Bring dim-sum during lunch hours, and Chinese pastries in the morning instead of doughnuts. (You might want to mix it up.)

- Always prepare many alternatives in order to give the Chinese negotiator room to negotiate several options with dignity.

- There is a Chinese custom of consulting a *feng shui* practitioner (a geomancer) to determine auspicious dates and special arrangements for opening new offices, moving, etc. When requested, this custom should be respected and observed. There are many issues that can be resolved in an efficient manner by respecting your Chinese counterpart's belief in the *feng shui* prophecies.

- Negotiation occurs over cups of tea. Always accept an offer of tea, whether you want it or not. When you are served, wait for the host to drink first.

Don'ts

- Don't mistake different Asian ancestries. For example, do not mistake a Korean person for Chinese. (Lee is a common last name for both ancestries.)

- Don't assume that the individual speaks Chinese or prefers to speak Chinese.

- Don't butcher names over and over again; it shows you are not trying. Ask the client to help you pronounce their name correctly.

- Avoid all of the following gifts and colors, which the Chinese associate with funerals:
  Straw sandals
  A stork or crane
  Handkerchiefs

Clock

Gift or wrapping paper in which the predominant color is white, black or blue

- Because the Chinese believe humility is a virtue, never exaggerate your ability to deliver.

- Don't talk down to your Chinese clients or sound like a know-it-all. It is better to let them show off than for you to do so.

- Don't use a Chinese person's first name until you have established a long-term relationship. Use an appropriate title in your salutation (e.g., Dr.) to show respect.

- Avoid making exaggerated gestures or using dramatic facial expressions. The Chinese do not typically use their hands when speaking, and they become distracted by a speaker who does.

- The Chinese do not usually like to be touched by people they do not know. This is especially important to remember when dealing with older people, those in important positions and females.

Historical Background

A significant aspect of China is its long cultural and national history. The Chinese people have shared a common culture longer than any other group on Earth. The Chinese writing system, for example, dates back almost 4,000 years. The imperial dynastic system of government, which continued for centuries, was established as early as 221 B.C. Although specific dynasties were overturned, the dynastic system survived. China was even ruled at times by foreign invaders—such as the Mongols during the Yuan Dynasty, from A.D. 1279 to 1368, and the Manchus during the Ch'ing Dynasty, from A.D. 1644 to 1911—but the foreigners were largely absorbed into the culture they governed.

The dynastic system was overturned in 1911, and a weak republican form of government existed until 1949. In that year, after a long civil war, the People's Republic of China was proclaimed, with a Communist government. This government and the ruling Communist Party have controlled China ever since. Although the dynastic system has disappeared, the People's Republic occupies essentially the same territory and governs the same people. If anything, the culture and power of China seem stronger in the late 20th century than at almost any other period in history. Under the People's Republic, China's role in world economic and political affairs has grown increasingly more important.

Immigration to the United States

The early Chinese came to the United States for many of the same reasons as European immigrants. There were years of famine and poverty in China. The United States offered the opportunity for work and the chance to send money home to one's family. Work in the California gold rush and the building of the transcontinental railroad offered the lamp of hope for many. The United States was known as *Gum San*, or Gold Mountain.

The Chinese were welcomed to work in California during the boom years of the mid-1800s.

There was a great need for labor and not enough hands. However, as the economic conditions changed for the worse, discrimination against the Chinese increased.

The first measure restricting immigration enacted by the U.S. Congress was a law, passed in 1862, forbidding American vessels to transport Chinese immigrants to the United States. Twenty years later, in 1882, as a byproduct of fear and ignorance, Congress passed the Chinese Exclusion Act.

In time, America began to realize that the treatment of Chinese immigrants was contrary to the philosophic foundations of the country. Awareness was raised by the protests and court challenges of Chinese Americans lobbying for their relatives who were still denied admittance. In 1943, the Chinese Exclusion Act was repealed allowing immigrants already in the United States to bring over family members from China. In 1952, the passage of the Walter-McCarren Act allowed first-generation Americans to apply for citizenship. Throughout the 1960s, Chinese Americans made particular gains into professional life. The 1964 Immigration and Nationality Act removed the last barriers to Chinese immigration, initiating a new era in the history of America's "melting pot".

Religion

Traditional Chinese thought is primarily shaped by Confucianism, a religion whose philosophy largely focuses on interpersonal and intergroup relationships. There also have been marginal influences from Buddhism and Daoism. A key virtue within all forms of Buddhism is the idea of compassion, and at the foundation of the Taoist belief system is the seeking of equilibrium in life. Chinese thought and religion, therefore, embody strong concern with human relations.

In the United States, many Chinese Americans are converting to different religions, primarily Protestantism or Catholicism. Like other ethnic minorities, Chinese Americans use the church for networking within the community.

The Chinese American Market

The Chinese American segment is the largest and most diverse group of all Asian-American markets in terms of political and cultural background, degrees of assimilation, and languages spoken. Chinese immigrants to the United States come from mainland China, Hong Kong (prior to its reunification with mainland China), Taiwan and Southeast Asia. The majority of Chinese Americans are first-generation immigrants, concentrated in major cities. Those born in the United States often refer to themselves as American-Born Chinese, using the acronym ABC.

Degree of Acculturation

Many Chinese are almost completely embedded in American life. However, a large percentage of first-generation immigrants are much less assimilated because of language problems.

Economic Status

Chinese immigrants challenged the United States to live up to the promise of equality and opportunity by resisting economic discrimination through class alliance within the community and with other ethnic groups. In this way, the Chinese corrected the perception that they were docile and servile.

The ethnic economy in most Chinatowns is characterized by the dominance of people from the same district or ancestral village in a specific occupation or business. This is because immigrants come from within a small geographical area, with many related by ingroup marriages, and partly because of their pattern of migration. This refers to chain migration, where the family members and friends who originally come from the same district or country migrate one after the other and possess a sense of regional solidarity. Members of the same district or county share this sense of regional solidarity

Holidays and Celebrations

The Chinese calendar is based on a combination of the lunar and solar calendars. It is calculated using the longitude of the sun and the phases of the moon. An ordinary year has 12 months and between 353 and 355 days. A leap year has 13 months and between 383 and 385 days. While the Chinese calendar is based on the phases of the moon, the Islamic and Hebrew calendars are based on the sighting of the first crescent. The Chinese lunar calendar, however, is based on the sighting of the new moon, or the completely "black moon".

The Chinese (Lunar) New Year: This is the biggest and most celebrated festival among the Chinese. Traditionally, families will begin cleaning their homes days before the New Year to sweep away ill fortune. A special dinner is served on New Year's Eve, and children and elders will receive gifts in the form of cash wrapped in red paper. One Chinese New Year tradition is the dragon or lion dance. The heads of these beasts are thought to ward off evil. The festival actually lasts several days, although the first few days are the most celebrated.

Chi'ng Ming, or *Qingming,* Festival (Ancestor Tribute): The festival, in which ancestors are revered and graves are cleaned, is usually celebrated in early April. It is considered unlucky to conduct important business on this day, or to have an operation. It is also believed that unhappy spirits, especially those with unfinished business, wander the Earth at this time. The holiday is officially observed in Hong Kong and Taiwan and is popular, though not official, in other countries where Chinese reside.

*Tuen Ng/*The Dragon Boat Festival: This holiday commemorates the attempt to rescue the patriotic poet Chu Yuan, who drowned on that day in 277 B.C. When they were unable to save him, the people threw bamboo stuffed with cooked rice into the water so that the fish would eat the rice rather than the body of their hero. To commemorate this, people eat *tzungtzu*, rice dumplings filled with ham or bean paste that has been wrapped in bamboo leaves. Traditional boat races on this day are meant to re-enact the attempted rescue of Chu Yuan. The boats are large canoes, usually highly decorated. Sticky stuffed rice balls wrapped in lotus leaves are a common treat during the festival. This holiday is celebrated on the fifth day of the fifth lunar month.

*Zhong Qiu Jie/*Moon Cake Festival (Mid-Autumn Festival): This holiday is second only to the Lunar New Year in significance. The moon on this day is the fullest and largest to the eye. The feature event of this holiday is for the whole family to view the moon while drinking wine and eating fruit and moon cakes. There is also a beautiful story that is a part of the festival. Children are told that there is a fairy on the moon living in a spacious but cold crystal palace with her sole companion, a jade rabbit. A heavenly general and friend occasionally pays her a visit, bringing along his fragrant wine. She then dances a beautiful dance. The shadows on the moon make the story all the more credible and fascinating to young imaginations.

The *Chung Yeung* Festival: Sometimes referred to as the double nine festival (because it falls on the ninth day of the ninth month on the Lunar Calendar). It is said that in 200 B.C., a man of the Han Dynasty avoided a catastrophe in his village by taking his family to a high place for the day. The man took with him food and a jug of chrysanthemum wine. This story has developed into a tradition whereby Chinese go picnicking in the mountains on this day. *Chung Yeung* is also a family remembrance day. Families visit graves to pay their respects to founding ancestors. They share the food they bring along, especially Chinese cakes called "ko", which is a homonym of the word for "top". It is also an auspicious time for the young and for lovers.

The Chinese Solar Year: The Chinese also make use of solar terms in their calendar. These are spaced at intervals of 15 degrees of solar longitude around the year and correspond closely to the entries and midpoints of the Western zodiac signs. At least within China, the date and time of each major and minor term are the points at which the solar longitude as observed at 120° East, an exact multiple of 15. The most important term from the calendar maker's point of view is the winter solstice, *Dongzhi*, which invariably falls in the 11th month and is used to determine the start of the Chinese year. Ancestors are venerated on *Dongzhi*.

NOTES

Cuban Americans

Cuban Americans
SUMMARY

Demographics

- The Cuban American population of the United States has increased 40 percent since 1990, from 1.04 million to 1.46 million in 2005.
- Close to half (46 percent) of Cuban Americans live in Florida. More than half (736,073, or 50.4 percent) of all Cuban Americans live in the state's Miami-Dade County.

Cultural Insights

- The ideas of political, personal and religious freedom and democracy are central to the Cuban American worldview.
- Sense of self is largely centered on one's position in the family and social group.
- Cuban exile status and struggle for freedom are central to Cuban American identity.
- Cuban Americans usually converse at a closer distance than the general population.
- Cuban Americans tend to be more relaxed and flexible about time and punctuality than non-Hispanics. Within the Hispanic community, not being on time is a socially acceptable behavior.
- Notions of interdependence, brotherhood and loyalty to one's peer group are strongly valued in Cuba. These values stand in sharp contrast to the independence and individualism of the United States.
- The Cuban government has stressed collective wealth and collective political awareness. People who have lived in the Cuban social system might be struck negatively by the materialism, winner-take-all capitalism, individualism, competition, crime and racism in the United States.
- While most other Hispanics in this country would classify themselves as Democrats, Cuban Americans are more likely to be politically conservative Republicans.
- *Machismo*, the idea that women are subordinate and inferior to men, is still a strong belief, but one that is consistently challenged.

Business Practices: Dos and Don'ts

Dos

- While punctuality is not necessarily a virtue among Cuban Americans, you should arrive on time to scheduled appointments.
- Particular attention should be given to gaining and maintaining trust, since personal relationships are generally important in business relationships.
- If possible, print business cards with English on one side and Spanish on the other.
- Dress to impress. Unacculturated Cuban Americans often give great importance to and place great value on looks and appearance as an indication of a sense of honor, dignity and pride.

- When approaching a group, attempt to greet and shake hands with as many people in the room as possible.

Don'ts

- Be careful not to refer to people from Cuba as Mexican.
- Avoid usage of racial categories that are common in the United States. A darker-skinned Cuban might not consider himself Black, as would a North American person of the same skin tone.
- Don't be impatient. The pace of business negotiations can be much slower.
- If invited to the home of an unacculturated Cuban for a meal, business should not be discussed. This should be treated as a social occasion. It is rude to leave food uneaten on your plate.
- While business can be discussed over lunch, it is uncommon to discuss business during dinner.
- Because personal relationships are so important, changing members of a sales team might be detrimental to business.

Cuban Americans

Demographics

According to the 2005 Census, the Cuban American population of the United States has increased 40 percent since 1990, from 1.04 million to 1.46 million.

The 10 most Cuban American populated states and territories in 2005 were:

1. Florida (1,000,151)
2. California (83,205)
3. New Jersey (77,451)
4. New York (66,687)
5. Texas (34,375)
6. Illinois (23,406)
7. Puerto Rico (20,251)
8. Georgia (19,049)
9. Nevada (14,759)
10. Pennsylvania (12,839)

The top Cuban American markets in the United States are:

1. Miami (736,073) *
2. New York (95,260) *
3. Tampa, Florida (14,674)
4. Los Angeles (12,431)

Including surrounding cities

Close to half (46 percent) of Cuban Americans live in Florida. More than half (736,073, or 50.4 percent) of those Cuban Americans live in the state's Miami-Dade County.

Cultural Insights

Worldview

- The ideas of political, personal and religious freedom and democracy are central to the Cuban American worldview.

- Collective empowerment is stressed among Cuban Americans.

Sense of Self

- Identity is largely centered on one's position in the family and social group.

- Exile status and the struggle for freedom are central to Cuban American identity.

Sense of Space

- Cuban Americans usually converse at a closer distance than the general population.

- There is a good deal more physical contact (e.g., touching of the arm, shoulder and lapel) than what is commonly seen in the general population. Thus, if possible and if you feel comfortable with this type of contact, try not to back away.

Communication Style

- Spanish speakers tend toward formality in their treatment of one another. A firm handshake is a common practice between people as a greeting and for leave-taking. A hug and a light kiss on the cheek are also common greeting practices between women, and men and women who are close friends or family.

- The Spanish language provides forms of formal and informal address (different use of *usted* vs. *tu* for the pronoun you, polite and familiar commands, and the use of titles of respect before people's first names, such as *Don* or *Doña*). In informal settings, conversations between Spanish speakers are usually loud and fast when compared to similar English- language conversations in the United States.

Eye Contact

- Maintaining eye contact is important. Looking away might project distrustfulness.

- Unacculturated Latinos also might avert their eyes in unpleasant or highly charged situations and confrontations.

Language

- The official and national language of Cuba is Spanish, which virtually all of the population speaks. Cuban Spanish is close to Puerto Rican and Dominican Spanish, but has special characteristics that make it easily identifiable. Spanish speakers from the Caribbean tend to speak faster than other Spanish speakers. In informal Cuban Spanish, for example, S is likely not to be pronounced, so you might hear *gracia* instead of *gracias*.

- In communities with significant numbers of Latinos, it is possible for Cubans to survive speaking little or no English. However, English is more and more becoming the preferred language of younger Cuban Americans. Those in professional positions will most likely be able to speak English as well as younger generations of immigrants. Many Cuban Americans are likely to speak Spanish at home, but are also able to speak English well.

Time and Time Consciousness

- Cuban Americans tend to be more relaxed and flexible about time and punctuality than non-Hispanics. Within the Hispanic community, not being on time is a socially acceptable behavior.

Values and Norms

- *Familismo* has to do with the high degree of interpersonal bonding within the Cuban family, resulting in greater identification with the group and dependence on the family. Recent studies also have demonstrated the importance of the nuclear and extended family as a source of social support. Latinos might "adopt" close friends as *compadres* and family members in the absence of blood ties.

- Respect for family is critical for Cuban Americans. The "family unit" includes not only parents and children, but also extended family. Families might be more rigidly structured. The father is the head of the family, and the mother is responsible for the home. Individuals within a family have a moral responsibility to aid other family members experiencing financial problems, unemployment, poor health conditions and other life challenges. Families often gather together to celebrate holidays, birthdays, baptisms, first communions, graduations and weddings. Cuban American families instill the importance of respect for authority and the elderly in their children.

- *Machismo* characterizes the male gender role in Latino society. It stresses virility, independence and physical strength. It supports the idea that women are subordinate and inferior to men. However, with more exposure to North American attitudes, this belief is being questioned.

- *Marianismo* has been characterized as the complement of *machismo*. *Marianismo* defines the role of the ideal woman, modeled after the Virgin Mary, as based on chastity, renunciation and sacredness, while reinforcing obedience.

- Any Cuban entrant to the United States younger than 50 years of age has spent most of his life in a country with an authoritarian, socialist, anti-American government. Even those coming to this country seeking personal and political freedoms might find the difference in values shocking.

- Notions of interdependence, brotherhood and loyalty to one's peer group are strongly valued in Cuba. These values stand in sharp contrast to the independence and individualism prevalent in the United States.

- Since it came to power, the socialist Cuban government has stressed collective wealth and collective political awareness. People who have lived in the Cuban social system might be struck negatively by the materialism, winner-take-all capitalism, individualism, competition, crime and racism in the United States.

- As a result of a socialist past, Cubans might see medical care, guaranteed employment, housing and education as basic rights, while North Americans have been taught that one has to work hard to achieve these privileges.

- As a consequence of living in a communist state, some Cuban newcomers might be oriented in the present and difficult to motivate to achieve long-term goals. However, many are highly resourceful. This contrast might reflect the contrast in Cuba between the official socialist system and the unofficial, who-you-know method of getting things done (called *sociolismo*, from the term *socio*, or "buddy").

- As with much of Latin America, ideologies of race are different in the United States and

Cuba. In the United States, color lines are rigid between Whites and non-Whites. Classification is not always as clear-cut among Cubans. Racial identity is more a question of physical appearance than biological descent, and classification depends largely on skin color and other visible characteristics, such as hair texture and the shape of the mouth or nose. Socioeconomic variables, such as occupation and education, also can affect a person's racial identity. A brown-skinned person who is well-educated might be referred to as White, while the same colored person who is not well-educated is more likely to be called *mulatto* or *moreno*. Because of the proliferation of multiple physical types, Cuba has not established a two-tiered system of racial discrimination.

- While most other Hispanics in this country would classify themselves as Democrats, Cuban Americans are more likely to be politically conservative Republicans.

- An interesting contrast regarding Cuban Americans is a relaxed attitude coupled with a strong drive for survival, success and accomplishment.

- In negotiations, the emotional impact of an interaction can be more important than the objective information and facts. Both trust and credibility must be established in order to build rapport. This is particularly important in the context of sales, where developing a relationship based on an emotional connection can make the difference between success and failure.

- Decisions will often favor friends and family over expertise.

Business Practices: Dos and Don'ts

Dos

- While punctuality is not necessarily a virtue among Cuban Americans, you should arrive on time to scheduled appointments.

- Particular attention should be given to gaining and maintaining trust, since personal relationships are generally important in business relationships.

- If possible, print business cards with English on one side and Spanish on the other.

- Dress to impress. Cuban Americans often give great importance to and place great value on looks and appearance as an indication of a sense of honor, dignity and pride.

- When approaching a group, attempt to greet and shake hands with as many people in the room as possible.

Don'ts

- The Hispanic population does not represent a single ethnic group; rather there are many Hispanic subgroups. Differences in educational levels, language skills, income and cultural values among Hispanics need to be considered. Even though Hispanics share the same language, their cultures might vary considerably. A common misperception is that all Hispanics are Mexican. Be careful not to refer to people from Cuba as Mexican.

- Avoid usage of racial categories that are common in the United States. A darker-skinned Cuban might not consider himself Black, as would a North American person of the same skin tone.

- Don't be impatient. The pace of business negotiations can be much slower.

- If invited to the home of an unacculturated Cuban for a meal, business should not be discussed. This should be treated as a social occasion. It is rude to leave food uneaten on your plate.

- While business can be discussed over lunch, it is uncommon to discuss business during dinner.

- Because personal relationships are so important, changing members of a sales team could be detrimental to business.

Historical Background

Similar to the other islands in the Caribbean, Cuba was originally populated by the agriculturalist Taino, a branch of the Arawak Indians. The native population was conquered by the Spanish after Columbus's arrival in 1492, and cattle ranching quickly became the mainstay of the Cuban economy. Large estates were established on the island under the *encomienda* system, enslaving the Indians under the pretext of offering instruction in Christianity. By 1542, only around 5,000 Indians (of an estimated 100,000 a half-century before) survived. The Spanish imported African slaves as replacements. Unlike the North American slave trade, Cuba's African slaves retained their tribal groupings and certain aspects of their culture endured.

Over the next few centuries, the Cuban economy expanded and, by the beginning of the 19th century, tobacco became one of the island's most important products. By 1820, Cuba was the world's largest sugar producer. After Mexican and South American independence, Cuba and Puerto Rico were the only remaining Spanish holdings in the Western Hemisphere. Spanish loyalists fled the former colonies and arrived in Cuba in droves. Even these settlers, however, began demanding home rule for the island, albeit under the Spanish flag.

Cuba launched its First War of Independence in 1868. After 10 years and 200,000 deaths, the rebels were spent and a pact was signed granting them amnesty. Meanwhile, a group of Cuban rebels exiled to the United States began plotting the overthrow of the Spanish colonial government. When the rebels landed in eastern Cuba in 1895, Spain retaliated with great force and re-established control (although with a more conciliatory approach).

During this time, U.S. interest in Cuba was growing. Many suspect that the U.S. government was behind the mysterious explosion of the U.S. warship *Maine*, which was anchored outside Havana Harbor and provided impetus for the Spanish-American War. The Spanish were defeated by the United States, and a peace treaty ending the war was signed Dec. 12, 1898.

Since U.S. law did not allow the government to annex Cuba outright, as it did Puerto Rico, Guam and the Philippines, the United States installed a governor, General John Brooke, and began a series of public works projects. These included building schools and improving public health. This further tied Cuba to the United States. In 1903, the United States built a naval base at Guantnamo Bay that is still in operation today.

By the 1920s, U.S. companies owned two-thirds of Cuba's farmland, imposing tariffs that crippled Cuba's own manufacturing industries. Discrimination against Blacks was institutionalized. Tourism based on drinking, gambling and prostitution flourished. The hardships of the Great Depression led to civil unrest, which was violently suppressed by President Gerado Machado y Morales. In 1933, Morales was overthrown in a coup, and army sergeant Fulgencio Batista seized power. Over the next 20 years, Cuba crumbled and its assets were increasingly placed into foreign hands. On Jan. 1, 1959, Batista's dictatorship was overthrown after a three-year guerilla campaign led by a young lawyer, Fidel Castro.

Castro was named prime minister and began reforming the nation's economy, cutting rents and nationalizing landholdings larger than 400 hectares. Relations with the United States deteriorated when he nationalized U.S.-owned petroleum refineries. The United States retaliated by cutting Cuban sugar imports, crippling the Cuban economy, and the CIA began plotting devious ways to overthrow the revolutionary government. Castro then turned to the Soviet Union, which promptly paid top dollar for Cuba's sugar surplus.

In 1961, 1,400 CIA-trained Cuban expatriates—mainly upper-middle-class Batista supporters who had fled to Miami after the revolution—attacked the island at the Bay of Pigs. They were promptly captured and ransomed back to the United States for medical supplies. The following week, Castro announced the socialist nature of the revolutionary government, something he'd always denied. The Soviet Union, was always eager to help a struggling socialist nation (particularly one so strategically located). Thus, they sent much-needed food, technical support and, of course, nuclear weapons. The October 1962 Cuban Missile Crisis is said to be the closest the world has ever come to nuclear conflict.

The missiles were shipped back to the U.S.S.R., and the United States declared a full-scale embargo on Cuba. Castro and his minister of economics, Che Guevara, began actively supporting guerilla groups in South America and Africa, sending troops and advisers to assist socialist insurgencies in Zaire, Angola, Mozambique, Bolivia (where Guevara was killed) and Ethiopia. The U.S. response was to support dictators in many of those countries. By the 1970s, Cuba limited its aid abroad; there were problems enough at home. Despite massive Soviet aid, the Cuban command economy was in ruins, and the country's plight worsened in 1989, when Russia withdrew its aid as Eastern Europe collapsed.

In December 1991, the Cuban Constitution was amended to remove all references to Marxism-Leninism, and economic reforms began. In 1993, laws were passed allowing Cubans to own and use U.S. dollars, to be self-employed and to open farmers' markets. Taxes on dollar incomes and profits were levied in 1994, and in September 1996, foreign companies were allowed to wholly own and operate businesses and purchase real estate. These measures gradually brought the economy out of its post-Soviet tailspin. The United States responded by stiffening its embargo with the Helms-Burton Act, ironically solidifying Castro's position as defender of Cuba against the evil empire.

74

The Cuban government has long been criticized for its human rights record. At least 500 people are "prisoners of conscience" for criticizing Cuba's present leadership or for attempting to organize political opposition. Each year, hundreds of Cubans brave shark-infested waters to come to the United States.

In November 1999, 6-year-old Elián González, whose mother died during that dangerous trip, made it to Miami by clinging to an inner tube. U.S. officials enforced a court order returning Elián to his father. In addition, bills that would relax the embargo—particularly regarding food and medicine, as well as travel restrictions between the countries—have a great deal of support in the U.S. Congress. These events might be a step toward reconciliation. As Castro's health declines, he has begun to pass the mantle of socialist revolutionary leader to Hugo Chavez of Venezuela.

Immigration to the United States

Given the closeness of Cuba to the United States, it is no surprise that there has always been movement of people between the countries. The Cuban American community now numbers almost 1½ million. The center of that community is in Miami, but there are sizable communities in other cities in Florida, as well as in New York, Illinois and California.

The existence and size of the Cuban American community in the United States is a result of both "push" and "pull" factors. The revolutionary government's inflexible attitude toward dissent, and its imperviousness to demands that dissenters make, probably constitute the greatest push factors. Another strong push factor for the recent wave of newcomers is the economic situation and scarcity of crucially necessary goods like medicine.

The pull factor has been the U.S. policy with regard to Cuban émigrés, which has effectively been, until recently, an unqualified welcome for both documented (Cubans entering the United States through normal immigration procedures, including legal departure from Cuba) and undocumented immigrants (Cubans arriving in the United States without immigrant visas, who have usually left Cuba illegally). Until 1985, there was no quota for Cubans entering the United States via normal immigration procedures, as there was for other immigrant groups. Cuban undocumented entrants have always had special status. While entrants from other countries have been required to demonstrate that they were fleeing political persecution to be granted refugee status, it was officially assumed that anyone arriving in the United States from Cuba was a bona fide refugee and, therefore, had automatic access to the special benefits to which refugees are entitled. Cuban entrants have had other special privileges, as well; since 1966, for example, the U.S. attorney general has had discretionary power to guarantee permanent residency to any Cuban who has been in the United States for a year, including those on visitor's visas who have overstayed the period delineated on their visas.

There have been, since the 1959 revolution, three primary waves of Cubans coming to the United States. These groups tend to differ from one another in their opinions and values, and have different acculturation experiences, depending partly on when and why they emigrated from Cuba, and partly on their reception in the United States. The first, from January 1959 to October 1962, comprised about 250,000 men and women (and their children) drawn from the business and professional classes. A few were associated with the Batista government. Between December 1965, and April 1973, another 400,000 people emigrated, this time from virtually all socioeconomic classes. Finally, in 1980, the Mariel boatlift produced a third wave nearly 120,000 people including many unskilled Cubans. A handful of common criminals and mental patients also arrived, but these were deliberately introduced by Castro to bedevil U.S. authorities and discredit the exile community as a whole.

Religion

Like most of Latin America, the Spanish imposed the Catholic religion on the population of Cuba. Eventually, Catholicism became the official and exclusive religion, although Castro would later declare Cuba to be an atheist nation. The vast majority of Cubans in the United States practice Catholicism. There are also growing numbers of Jewish and Protestant Cuban Americans.

The influence of the African presence in Cuba is apparent with the practice of Santería (Way of the Saints). Santería, a religion practiced throughout the Caribbean, combines the beliefs of the Yoruba, or Bantu, people of Africa with elements of worship from Roman Catholicism. The original name of the religion was Lucumí, or La Regla Lucum . Santería was a derogatory term used by the Spanish to describe the religious practices of the slaves and peasantry. It is only relatively recently that members of the religion have used the term. With Santería, people approach God through intermediaries, such as the clergy, saints, witches (*brujos*) and healers (*curanderos*). *Curanderos* consult the saints to ascertain which herbs, roots and various home cures to employ. *Brujos* also provide cures by driving out spirits that sometimes possess an individual. Currently, it is estimated that in Cuba, as much as 70 percent of the population adheres to some form of Afro-Cuban beliefs. In the United States, Santería is practiced by a select, and often isolated, few.

The Cuban American Market

Cuban Americans are among the most successful of the Latino population. This is largely because of selective migration. Initial waves of immigrants were, on average, well-educated professionals and were able to establish a solid economic foundation for subsequent groups. Cuban Americans provide a good example of why relative economic success does not necessarily translate into an assimilated group. Cuban American businesspeople have been largely dependent on their co-ethnic communities for support, and their communities provide them with a source of economic and political empowerment.

Degree of Acculturation

As with most immigrant groups, later generations of Cuban Americans have become more acculturated into U.S. mainstream culture than first-generation immigrants. Cuban Americans, however, have steadfastly held onto their customs, traditions and language. This is especially true where there are large populations of Cuban Americans and the population is consistently renewed with recently arrived immigrants. It might also have to do with the (now declining) idea that they are exiles as opposed to immigrants, and that someday it will be possible to return to Cuba.

Holidays and Celebrations

For nearly 30 years, there was no Christmas in Cuba. It has only been relatively recently that the

Cuban government has allowed the practice of religion and the observance of religious holidays like Christmas. In the United States, however, Cuban Americans take part in all U.S. holidays, including those of a religious nature, and celebrations are similar to those of non-immigrants.

Año Nuevo (New Year's Day) — Jan. 1: Traditional Western holiday.

Day of the Magi/Day of the Three Kings (_Día de los Santos Reyes/Magos_)—Jan. 6: Traditionally, it is the day when gifts are dispensed (as opposed to Christmas Day) to commemorate the day when the Magi presented gifts to Jesus of Nazareth. This day is celebrated differently among different Latino groups in the United States and is losing some of its significance with the increased focus on Christmas, but it is mostly considered a day for children to receive gifts and celebrate.

El Festival de la Ocho (Calle Ocho Festival)—Mid-March: This festival in Miami is known as the "world's largest block party" and is held along 23 blocks in Little Havana. The celebration marks the end of the ten-day-long Carnival.

Hispanic Heritage Month—Sept. 15-Oct. 15: A month designated by the U.S. government to celebrate and explore Latino history and influence in this country.

Christmas Eve (_Nochebuena_) and Christmas (_Navidad_)—Dec. 24-25: Christmas Eve (December 24) is widely observed, and dinner and festivities take place on this day, rather than Dec. 25.

_Quinceañera_s: A _quinceañera_, or 15th-birthday celebration, is a rite of passage for young Catholic Hispanic girls, and is growing in popularity in the United States. The roots of the ceremony are found in a combination of indigenous and Spanish customs, and it is meant to represent a girl's emergence into womanhood. Girls are required to attend a year of religion classes before the celebration, which usually begins with a Mass followed by a party. The celebration itself tends be very extravagant, and can rival a wedding in nature. The girl will wear an elaborate dress that symbolizes femininity, a gold medallion that expresses her faith, a ring that represents her spiritual and communal responsibilities, and a crown that symbolizes her living a Christian life. She will have 14 maids of honor, or _damas_ (one for each year of childhood), and each will have a male escort—all of whom will perform a symbolic dance for the occasion. These events can cost thousands of dollars, and friends and relatives will often help with expenses. This celebration had its roots with the Mexican population, but its popularity and practice has spread to other Latino groups in the United States.

NOTES

Dominican Americans

Dominican Americans
SUMMARY

Demographics

- The Dominican population of the United States was 1,118,265 in 2005. The population has increased 115 percent from a 1990 total of 520,151.
- The Dominican Republic is one of the largest sources of new Hispanic immigrants to New York City.

Cultural Insights

- The Trujillo Era has left an indelible mark on the identity of Dominicans. Political freedom and justice are central to the Dominican worldview.
- Self-identity is largely centered on one's position in the family and social group.
- Dominicans might converse at a closer distance than North Americans.
- Dominicans tend to be more relaxed and flexible about time and punctuality than non-Hispanics. Within the Hispanic community, not being on time is a socially acceptable behavior.
- Respect for family is critical for Dominicans. The "family unit" includes not only parents and children but also extended family. Families might be more rigidly structured: The father is the head of the family, and the mother is responsible for the home. Individuals within a family have a moral responsibility to aid other family members who are experiencing financial problems, unemployment, poor health conditions and other life issues. Families often gather together to celebrate holidays, birthdays, baptisms, first communions, graduations and weddings. Dominican families instill in their children the importance of respect for authority and the elderly.
- Homeland politics are important to Dominican immigrants. Each political party in the Dominican Republic has headquarters in Washington Heights, where most Dominican New Yorkers live.
- It is often said that baseball and politics are the two loves of Dominicans. This population is extremely proud of the presence of Dominicans in Major League Baseball.

Business Practices: Dos and Don'ts

Dos

- While punctuality is not necessarily a virtue among many Dominicans, it is always best to arrive on time to scheduled appointments. If possible, allow extra time for meetings.
- Particular attention should be given to gaining and maintaining trust, because personal relationships are generally important in business relationships.
- If possible, print business cards with English on one side and Spanish on the other.
- Dress well. Dominicans often give great importance to and place great value on looks and appearance as conveying a sense of honor, dignity and pride.

- When approaching a group, attempt to greet and shake hands with everybody in the room.

Don'ts

- The Hispanic population does not represent a single ethnic group; rather there are many Hispanic subgroups. Differences in education levels, language skills, income levels and cultural values among Hispanics need to be considered. Even though Hispanics share the same language, their cultures might vary considerably. Do not assume that all Hispanics are Mexican.
- Try to avoid usage of racial categories that are common in the United States. A darker-skinned Dominican might not consider himself Black, as would a North American person of the same skin tone.
- Don't be impatient. The pace of business negotiations can be much slower.
- If invited to the home of an unacculturated Dominican for a meal, business should not be discussed—it should be treated as a social occasion. It is rude to leave food uneaten on your plate.
- While business can be discussed over lunch, it is uncommon to discuss business during dinner.
- Because personal relationships are so important, changing members of a negotiation team might bring business to a halt.

Dominican Americans

Demographics

According to the 2005 American Community Survey, the Dominican population of the United States was 1,118,265. The population increased 115 percent from a 1990 total of 520,151. (Many demographers feel that the actual Dominican population is probably double this number.)

The five most Dominican populated states in 2005 were (NA indicates that exact population figures are not available):

1. New York (602,285)
2. New Jersey (159,118)
3. Florida (121,675)
4. Massachusetts (81,136)
5. Connecticut (NA)

In 2005, 602,285 Dominicans lived in the state of New York. The majority (88 percent) lived in New York County (165,260), Bronx County (204,401), Queens County (81,611) and Kings County (78,909).

Currently, the Dominican Republic is one of the largest sources of new Hispanic immigrants to New York City.

Cultural Insights

Worldview

- The Trujillo Era has left an indelible mark on the identity of Dominicans. Political freedom and justice are central to the Dominican worldview.

- Dominicans are said to live for the present but value the past.

Sense of Self

- Self-identity is largely centered on one's position in the family and social group.

Sense of Space

- Dominicans might converse at a closer distance than North Americans.

- There might be a good deal more physical contact (e.g., touching of the arm, shoulder and lapel), so try not to back away.

Communication Style

- Spanish speakers tend toward formality in their treatment of one another. A firm handshake is a common practice between people as greeting and for leave-taking. A hug and a light kiss on the cheek are also common greeting practices between women, and men and women who are close friends or family.

- The Spanish language provides forms of formal and non-formal address (different use of *usted* vs. *tu* for the pronoun you, polite and familiar commands, and the use of titles of respect before people's first names such as *Don* or *Doña*). This indicates the importance of being respectful and maintaining a proper social distance, especially among elders or people accorded a higher status. In non-formal settings, conversations between Spanish speakers are usually loud and fast when compared to similar English-language conversations in the United States.

- In non-formal settings, conversations between Spanish speakers can be louder and faster than is the custom among the majority populations in the United States.

Eye Contact

- Maintaining eye contact is important. Looking away might project that you are unworthy of trust. However, among people from rural areas or with less education and social status, lack of eye contact might indicate a sign of respect.

- Unacculturated Latinos also might avert their eyes in unpleasant or highly charged situations and confrontations.

Language

- The official and national language of the Dominican Republic is Spanish, which virtually all of the population speaks. The Dominican accent is similar to other Caribbean-based Spanish populations.

- In communities with significant numbers of Latinos, it is possible for Dominicans to survive speaking little or no English. Most Dominicans, especially business professionals and those born in the United States, have the ability to speak English well, although they are still highly likely to speak Spanish at home.

Time and Time Consciousness

- Dominicans tend to be more relaxed and flexible about time and punctuality than non-Hispanics. Within the Hispanic community, not being on time is a socially acceptable behavior.

Values and Norms

- *Familismo* has to do with the high degree of interpersonal bonding within the Dominican family, resulting in greater identification with the group and dependence on the family.

Recent studies also have demonstrated the importance of the nuclear and extended family as a source of social support. Latinos might "adopt" close friends as *compadres* and family members in the absence of blood ties.

- *Machismo* characterizes the male gender role in Latino society. It stresses virility, independence and physical strength. It supports the idea that women are subordinate and inferior to men. However, with more exposure to North American attitudes, this belief is being questioned.

- *Marianismo* has been characterized as the complement of *machismo*. *Marianismo* defines the role of the ideal woman, modeled after the Virgin Mary, as based on chastity, renunciation and sacredness, while reinforcing obedience.

- Respect for family is critical for Dominicans. The "family unit" includes not only parents and children but also extended family. Families might be more rigidly structured: The father is the head of the family, and the mother is responsible for the home. Individuals within a family have a moral responsibility to aid other members of the family experiencing financial problems, unemployment, poor health conditions and other life issues. Families often gather together to celebrate holidays, birthdays, baptisms, first communions, graduations and weddings. Dominican families instill in their children the importance of respect for authority and the elderly.

- As with much of Latin America, ideologies of race are different in the United States and the Dominican Republic. In the United States, color lines are rigid between Whites and non-Whites. Due to extensive race mixing in the past and the variety of colors that characterize the Dominican population, dark skin color does not necessarily assign one to a politicized or racialized group in the Dominican Republic. At the same time, dark skin is often considered unattractive and accorded a lesser status than lighter skin. Also, to be Black in the Dominican Republic is often negatively associated with being a native of Haiti, a country toward which Dominicans hold much animosity. Color classification in the country depends largely on skin color and other visible characteristics, such as hair texture and the shape of the mouth and nose. Socioeconomic variables, such as occupation and education, also can affect a person's color identity. A brown-skinned person who is well-educated might be referred to as White, while the same colored person who is not well-educated is more likely to be called *mulatto* or *moreno*.

- Homeland politics are important to Dominican immigrants. Each political party in the Dominican Republic has headquarters in Washington Heights, where most Dominican New Yorkers live.

- It is often said that baseball and politics are the two loves of Dominicans. This population is extremely proud of the presence of Dominicans in Major League Baseball.

- In negotiations, the emotional impact of an interaction can be more important than the objective information and facts. This is particularly important in the context of sales, where developing a relationship based on an emotional connection can mean the difference between success and failure.

- Business decisions are heavily impacted by personal relationships.

Business Practices: Dos and Don'ts

Dos

- While punctuality is not necessarily a virtue among many Dominicans, it is always best to arrive on time to scheduled appointments. If possible, allow extra time for meetings.

- Particular attention should be given to gaining and maintaining trust, because personal relationships are generally important in business relationships.

- If possible, print business cards with English on one side and Spanish on the other.

- Dress well. Dominicans often give great importance to and place great value on looks and appearance as a sense of honor, dignity and pride.

- When approaching a group, attempt to greet and shake hands with everybody in the room.

Don'ts

- The Hispanic population does not represent a single ethnic group; rather there are many Hispanic subgroups. Differences in education levels, language skills, income levels and cultural values among Hispanics need to be considered. Even though Hispanics share the same language, their cultures might vary considerably. Do not assume that all Hispanics are Mexican.

- Try to avoid usage of racial categories that are common in the United States. A darker-skinned Dominican might not consider himself Black, as would a North American person of the same skin tone.

- Don't be impatient. The pace of business negotiations can be much slower.

- If invited to the home of an unacculturated Dominican for a meal, business should not be discussed—it should be treated as a social occasion. Among the unacculturated, it is rude to leave food uneaten on your plate.

- While business can be discussed over lunch, it is uncommon to discuss business during dinner.

- Because personal relationships are so important, changing members of a negotiation team might bring business to a halt.

Historical Background

The aboriginal inhabitants of Hispaniola were Arawak people, engaged principally in farming and fishing. They eventually became extinct as a result of exploitation by Spanish colonists and the diseases they brought to the New World. Black slaves were later imported to take the place of the Arawak laborers. In time, the Spanish migrated from Hispaniola to South America, and for about a century the island was sparsely populated. In the late 17th century, French adventurers began to explore part of the island. In 1697, that portion of Hispaniola was formally ceded to France and became known as Saint Dominique; it is now Haiti. The remaining Spanish section—that is now the Dominican Republic—was called Santo Domingo.

The French developed a successful plantation economy on their side of the island, while the Spanish area declined; many people left, and much of the land remained unpopulated. Spain finally ceded Santo Domingo to France in 1795. During the years that followed, the country was caught up in the convulsions of neighboring nascent Haiti, fought over by the French, Spanish and English, as well as indigenous mixed-race and Black people. When Haiti ousted the French in 1804, Santo Domingo remained under French occupation for another five years. Then the French were expelled, and nominal Spanish rule was restored.

After 1814, however, the Spanish administration became increasingly tyrannical and in 1821, the Dominicans rose in revolt, proclaiming their independence. Independence was short-lived. The following year, Haitian troops marched into the country and annexed it to Haiti, thus bringing the entire island under Haitian control. The Haitians were overthrown by a revolution in 1844. A year later, Santo Domingo again declared its independence, forming the Dominican Republic.

The following years were characterized by internal strife. Between 1861 and 1863, the country returned to Spanish rule. Independence was reclaimed by 1865. Economic problems forced the country to sign a fifty-year treaty with the United States. Eventually, the United States Marines established a military government in the country. By March 1924, Dominicans once again gained control of their country.

Rafael Leonidas Trujillo Molina was elected to the presidency in 1930 by forcibly eliminating all opposition. For the next 31 years, although he personally occupied the presidency only half that time (from 1930 to 1938 and again from 1943 to 1952), Trujillo presided over one of the most rigid dictatorships in the world. Backed at first by the United States, Trujillo used this support to his own advantage in shoring up power. Discontent and criticism were widespread, especially after the end of World War II in 1945. The Trujillo Era is perhaps best known as one of complete terror for Haitians and Haitian descendents living in the Dominican Republic. During Trujillo's rise to power, however, considerable material progress was made.

The Trujillo Era ended with the dictator's assassination on May 26, 1961. Numerous exiles began to return home, and political parties were re-established. In October 1961, the two brothers of the late dictator left the country, but they returned in November, apparently with the intention of seizing governmental power. President Joaquín Balaguer, who had assumed the office as a Trujillo puppet in 1960, reacted to the threat by assuming control of the armed forces. Supported by the United States, the show of force speedily induced all members of the Trujillo family to leave the country. Opposition groups, however, rallied against Balaguer; after a wave of strikes and demonstrations, he and his opponents agreed on a plan under which he would retain the presidency until sanctions imposed by the Organization of American States were lifted.

In December 1962, the Dominican Republic held its first free election in nearly four decades. Juan Bosch, a returned exile, won by a wide margin and was inaugurated on Feb. 27, 1963. Almost immediately, opposition to his regime began to develop. Bosch was criticized as being too tolerant of pro-Castro and communist groups, and the business community felt threatened by changes in the country's economic policy. On Sept. 25, Bosch was deposed by a military coup and the leaders installed a three-man civilian junta. To indicate disapproval of the coup, the United States withheld recognition until the new regime promised to hold elections by 1965.

Throughout 1964, restlessness within the country was manifested by strikes and sabotage and by conflicts within the junta. Marines were stationed in Santo Domingo to protect U.S. interests. Eventually, a provisional government was established and in June 1966, Balaguer, a conservative, won with 56 percent of the vote. Under his administration, although not completely democratic, relative stability was restored to the country. The economy showed strength, aided by high sugar prices, foreign investment and increased tourism, enabling Balaguer to win re-election easily in 1970 and 1974. Balaguer lost the presidency in 1978 and regained it in 1986. In a presidential runoff election held in June 1996, Leonel Fernndez Reyna defeated José Francisco Peña Gómez to win the presidency of the Dominican Republic.

Immigration to the United States

Dominicans did not establish a significant presence in the United States until after the 1960s. This was most likely because of two factors: the high cost of migration and travel restrictions imposed by the Trujillo regime. It was with Trujillo's assassination in 1961 that the first significant wave of migration (primarily to New York) began. With Trujillo's death came the demise of his emigration restrictions, and U.S. consular officials, concerned about leftwing turbulence on the island, also made it much easier for potential exiles to leave.

Six out of ten Dominicans who immigrated to the United States moved to New York City. Dominican immigrants depended on earlier settlers. Specifically, they depended on earlier waves of Puerto Ricans who had created niches in the garment, hotel, restaurant and light manufacturing industries. The new immigrants filled the gaps in the low-skilled sector that older immigrants and Blacks would not. By 1970, they had established niches in the apparel and restaurant industries.

As economic conditions in the Dominican Republic worsened, particularly in the 1980s and 1990s, Dominican immigration to the United States soared. Today, Dominicans rank high among the foreign-born population of the country. While there has been some economic progress for Dominicans, that progress has been relatively modest and Dominicans continue to be over-represented in low-paying, dead-end jobs.

Religion

The majority of Dominican Americans profess Roman Catholicism, although few actually attend Mass regularly. Popular religions in the Dominican Republic were often far removed from the Roman Catholic orthodoxy and heavily influenced by African and indigenous cultural practices. For example, Santería, a religion practiced throughout the Caribbean, combines the beliefs of the Yoruba or Bantu people with elements of worship from Roman Catholicism. The original name of the religion was Lucumí or La Regla Lucumí. Santería was a derogative term used by the Spanish to describe the religious practices of the slaves and peasantry. It is only recently that members of the religion have used the term. With Santería, people approach God through intermediaries—the clergy, the saints, witches (*brujos*), and healers (*curanderos*). The saints play an important role in popular devotion. *Curanderos* consult the saints to ascertain which herbs, roots and various home cures to employ. Witches (*brujos*) also cure by driving out spirits that sometimes seize and possess an individual.

Degree of Acculturation

Dominicans are relatively new immigrants to the United States. Older immigrants are still closely tied to their homeland. In New York, for example, many organize support and raise money for political candidates in the Dominican Republic. Many parents might choose to send their children to high school in the Dominican Republic. Younger Dominicans tend to be more concerned with empowering the Dominican community in this country. Darker-skinned Dominicans deal with acculturation on several levels, because they must adapt to both White America and Black America. Either way, community ties remain strong and being Dominican is still a major part of their identity. In fact, Dominicans in New York are often referred to as Dominican Yorks.

Economic Status

Upon arrival, Dominicans have largely found work in low-skill, low-wage jobs. The situation has not improved. In fact, some studies report that their situation has worsened and almost half live below the poverty line. This is likely because of several factors: a lack of low-skill manufacturing jobs for new immigrants, low levels of education, and high numbers of recent immigrants.

Holidays and Celebrations

Dominican Americans celebrate all U.S. holidays. The most important holidays include New Year's Day, Good Friday, Easter and Christmas.

Año Nuevo (New Year's Day)—Jan. 1: Traditional Western holiday.

Day of the Magi/Day of the Three Kings (*Día de los Santos Reyes/Magos*)—Jan. 6: Traditionally, it is this day when gifts are dispensed (as opposed to Christmas Day) to commemorate the day when the Magi presented gifts to Jesus of Nazareth. This day is celebrated differently among different Latino groups in the United States and is losing some of its significance with the increased focus on Christmas, but it is mostly considered a day for children to receive gifts and celebrate.

Easter and *La Semana Santa* (Holy Week): Easter is one of the highest holy days of the year for Latino Catholics. It is celebrated nearly everywhere in Latin America and Spain with religious observances and various types of processions. *Semana Santa* begins with Palm Sunday (*el Domingo de Ramos*), includes Good Friday (*el Viernes Santo*) and ends with Easter (*la Pascua de Resurrección*). The week is meant to mark the triumphant entry of Jesus into Jerusalem, followed by his death and resurrection.

Hispanic Heritage Month—Sept. 15-Oct. 15: A month designated by the U.S. government to celebrate and explore Latino history and influence in this country.

Christmas Eve (*Nochebuena*) and Christmas (*Navidad*)—Dec. 24-25: Christmas Eve (Dec. 24) is widely observed, and dinner and festivities take place on this day, rather than Dec. 25.

Quinceañeras: A *quinceañera*, or 15th-birthday celebration, is a rite of passage for young, Catholic Hispanic girls, and is growing in popularity in the United States. The roots of the ceremony are found in a combination of indigenous and Spanish customs, and it is meant to represent a girl's emergence into womanhood. Girls are required to attend a year of religion classes before the celebration, which usually begins with a Mass followed by a party. The celebration itself tends be extravagant, and can rival a wedding in nature. The girl will wear an elaborate dress that symbolizes femininity, a gold medallion that expresses her faith, a ring that represents her spiritual and communal responsibilities and a crown that symbolizes her living a Christian life. She will have 14 maids of honor, or *damas* (one for each year of childhood), and each will have a male escort—all of whom will perform a symbolic dance for the occasion. These events can cost thousands of dollars, and friends and relatives will often help with the expenses.

NOTES

Filipino Americans

Filipino Americans
SUMMARY

Demographics

- According to the 2005 Census, there are 2,282,872 Filipino Americans living in the United States. They are the third-largest Asian group in the United States, following the Chinese and Asian Indians.
- The most Filipino-populated state is California, followed by Hawaii. The largest Filipino market is Los Angeles, followed by Honolulu and San Diego.

Cultural Insights

- Culturally, Filipinos are unique. The majority of Filipinos are Malay, Roman Catholic (this is the only Christian nation in Asia), have Hispanic surnames and speak some English. The Philippines is the fourth-largest English-speaking country in the world, after the United States, the United Kingdom and India.
- Avoiding one's own embarrassment and the embarrassment of others is a key component in Filipino interactions. Smiles might hide embarrassment and discord.
- Important Filipino American holidays and celebrations include Christmas, Philippine Independence Day, Rizal Day and Filipino-American Friendship Day.

Business Practices: Dos and Don'ts

Dos

- In the Philippines, it is traditional to have a letter of introduction for important business transactions. However, in the United States this practice has been replaced by telling your business counterpart that you were referred by common friends or business associates.
- Be humble. Filipinos consider everyone worthy of respect. The more important and intelligent you are, the more you are expected to be humble and generous.
- Social contacts are more important among Filipino Americans than business ones. An unacculturated Filipino must like you and be comfortable with you in order to do meaningful business.

Don'ts

- Never decline an invitation to a social event. Expect to see your Filipino business partners often at social situations.
- Don't be overly aggressive. Speak in quiet, gentle tones. Filipino Americans revere harmony. The only time they would be loud is when they are boisterously happy.
- Pointing with fingers can easily be taken for an insulting gesture. Filipino Americans rarely indicate objects or directions by pointing with their fingers. Instead, they indicate with a glance or by pursing their lips.

Filipino Americans

Demographics

According to the 2005 Census, there are 2,282,872 Filipino Americans living in the United States. They are the third-largest Asian group in the country, following the Chinese and Asian Indians.

The 10 most Filipino populated states are:

1. California (1,085,868)
2. Hawaii (185,029)
3. New Jersey (110,817)
4. Illinois (103,363)
5. New York (100,363)
6. Washington (87,871)
7. Texas (87,384)
8. Florida (80,660)
9. Nevada (72,277)
10. Virginia (59,179)

The top 10 Filipino markets in the United States in 2005 were (NA indicates that exact population figures are not available):

1. Los Angeles (363,810) *
2. Honolulu (161,568) *
3. San Diego (136,845) *
4. New York (125,551) *
5. San Francisco (124,749) *
6. Chicago (97,756) *
7. Seattle/Tacoma (NA) *
8. Sacramento CA (NA) *
9. Washington DC (NA) *
10. Houston (NA)

Includes surrounding cities

Cultural Insights

Worldview

- Filipino Americans have a strong sense of family and cultural/community preservation.

- Filipino Americans are a gentle, friendly and cheerful people, noted for their courtesy and hospitality.

Sense of Self

- Individuals act in the context of the group. Decisions typically are not made without consensus.

Sense of Space

- The unique culture of the Philippines, which stems from the mixture of Western and Asian cultures along with the gentle nature of the Filipinos, has lessened the need for distance in personal interactions.

96

Communication Style

- In their language and mannerisms, Filipinos frequently show a great deal of respect to their elders.

- Filipinos might smile or laugh in situations that Westerners consider inappropriate. Smiles hide embarrassment and discord. Thus, Filipino businessmen might laugh during the most serious part of a business meeting.

Eye Contact

- Among Filipinos, much can be communicated via eye contact and eyebrow movement. Filipinos might greet each other by making eye contact followed by a raising and lowering of the eyebrows.

- Avoid staring. This can be interpreted as belligerence.

Language

- The Philippines is a nation of many languages and dialects, all of which belong to the Malay-Polynesian family of languages.

- Of the eight principal native languages used in the Philippines, Cebuano is the most widely spoken of the dialects. It is used by about 24.5 percent of the population. Tagalog, which is commonly spoken by U.S. Filipinos, ranks a close second (approximately 24 percent), followed by Ilocano (11 percent).

- English is the language of instruction in schools, but Filipino (often pronounced as Pilipino with a "P" sound because there is no "F" sound in their language) is the national language. Much of Filipino is derived from the Tagalog dialect spoken in Manila and nearby provinces.

- English is the most widely used language in the country, especially for education, commerce and the professions.

- According to the 2000 Census, Filipinos in the United States are the least dependent of any Asian immigrant group on their native language. In other words, fewer Filipino households in the United States have members who do not speak English at all, and more Filipino households have members who rate themselves as speaking English very well.

- Unlike many other Asian groups, many Filipino immigrants are familiar with English as soon as they arrive in the United States. As a matter of fact, the Philippines is the fourth-largest English-speaking country in the world, after the United States, the United Kingdom and India. This is because of the introduction of the U.S. public education system in the Philippines in the early 20th century, after the Spanish-American War. That is when the Phillipines became a colony of the United States. Thus, starting in first grade, English became the medium of instruction in the schools. Given the many different languages and dialects spoken, English became a unifying force in the country. Until recently, it also was the main form of communication in Filipino governmental affairs.

Time and Time Consciousness

- Filipino Americans tend to be reasonably punctual for business meetings.

- Social events often do not start at the stated time. It might be impolite to arrive on time to a party (with the exception of weddings).

Values and Norms

- Culturally, Filipinos are unique. The majority of Filipinos are Malay, Roman Catholic (this is the only Christian nation in Asia), have Hispanic surnames and speak some English.

- It is important for Filipinos to avoid embarrassing others or being embarrassed themselves.

- Personal honor, respect for the aged, proper courtship behavior and appropriate demeanor remain important among most Filipino Americans.

- Filipinos value the virtue of helping each other and other people. They cherish the ancestral trait of *bayanihan,* which means cooperation and the spirit of community, town or nation. The concept of a group of people working together toward a common goal is most clearly portrayed by the historic Filipino custom of many volunteers cooperatively moving a home to a new location using a bamboo frame.

Business Practices: Dos and Don'ts

Dos

- In the Philippines, it is traditional to have a letter of introduction for important business transactions. However, in the United States this practice has been replaced by telling your business counterpart that you were referred by common friends or business associates.

- Be humble. Filipinos consider everyone worthy of respect. The more important and intelligent you are, the more you are expected to be humble and generous.

- Social contacts are more important with Filipino Americans than business ones. A Filipino, usually, must like you and be comfortable with you in order to do significant business.

Don'ts

- Never decline an invitation to a social event.

- Don't be overly aggressive. Speak in quiet, gentle tones. Filipino Americans revere harmony. Typically, the only time they would be loud is when they are boisterously happy.

98

Historical Background

The first inhabitants of the Philippines arrived up to 300,000 years ago, probably migrating over a land bridge from the Asian mainland. The Negrito or Aeta arrived 25,000 years ago, but they were displaced by several waves of immigrants from Indonesia. This was followed by maritime immigrations of Malayan people. In 1380, the Arab-taught Makdum arrived in the Sulu archipelago and began to establish what became a powerful Islamic sphere of influence. It lasted for the next hundred years.

Ferdinand Magellan landed in 1521 and claimed the archipelago for Spain. Magellan was killed by local chiefs who quite naturally disapproved of this notion. Ruy Lopez de Villalobos followed in 1543 and named the territory Filipinas after Philip II of Spain. Permanent Spanish occupation began in 1565. By 1571, the entire country—except for the strictly Islamic Sulu archipelago— was under Spanish control. Similar to the indigenous populations of Latin America, the Filipinos experienced a class-based society and coincident exclusion under Spanish domination.

A Filipino independence movement grew in the 19th century, and Filipinos fought on the side of the Americans in 1898 during the Spanish-American War. When the Spanish were defeated, General Aguinaldo declared the Philippines independent. The United States, however, had other plans. They promptly purchased the islands from the Spanish for $20 million. Filipinos rebelled against U.S. domination. This rebellion was put down with the loss of many thousands of lives, and the Philippines remained a U.S. colony.

The United States eventually recognized the Filipinos desire for independence, and Manuel L. Quezon was sworn in as president of the Philippine Commonwealth in 1935 as part of a transitional phase pending full independence. Japan brutally interrupted this process, invading the Philippines in 1942 and ruling until the U.S. invasion two years later. The Philippines received full independence in 1946.

Immigration to the United States

Filipinos were some of the first Asians ever to cross the Pacific Ocean and set foot on North American soil. From 1565 to 1815, during the Manila-Acapulco Galleon Trade, Filipinos came to America working as the sailors and navigators on board Spanish ships.

The first wave of Filipino immigration into the United States began in the late 1700s. In 1763, Filipinos made their first permanent settlement in the bayous and marshes of Louisiana. These immigrants were sailors and navigators, Filipinos who jumped ship to escape the brutality of their Spanish masters. They built houses and settled in and around New Orleans.

The second wave of Filipino immigration to the United States lasted from 1906 to 1934, with a heavy concentration settling in California and Hawaii. In California, they worked many long hours on farms and in the agricultural fields picking fruits and vegetables in places like Hayward, Salinas, Stockton, El Centro and Escondido. In Alaska, they worked in the fish canneries.

The third wave of Filipino immigration into the United States began during WWII, when Filipinos were allowed to join the U.S. Navy to fight against Japan. Joining the Navy became a common means for Filipinos to immigrate to the United States. They were not considered U.S.

citizens, nor were they illegal aliens.

The fourth wave of Filipino immigration began after the passing of the Immigration Act of 1965 and continues to the present day. This allowed the entry of as many as 20,000 Filipino immigrants annually. This wave of Filipinos was also called the brain drain. It consisted mainly of professionals: doctors, lawyers, nurses and engineers, as well as military personnel.

Religion

Here in the United States, religion has continued to be an important part of Filipino life. Like most Americans, the majority of Filipinos in the United States are Christian. Most, in fact, are Roman Catholic. This is largely because of 350 years of Spanish colonial rule when Spanish friars converted Filipinos to Christianity. Some Filipino Americans are Muslim, and a few are Protestant.

For many Filipinos, the rituals of the Catholic Church are times for religious ceremony as well as a social celebration.

The Filipino American Market

In 2005, the U.S. Census showed that about 60 percent of the overall Filipino population, both foreign and native-born, resided on the West Coast (California and Washington) and in Hawaii. They mostly resided in Los Angeles, San Francisco and Honolulu. However, there are signs of growing Filipino population in the large urban areas of the East Coast, with the largest concentrations in Illinois, New York, Washington, D.C., and New Jersey.

Filipino Americans today are an important emerging Asian ethnic group. They are currently the third-largest Asian population after Chinese and Indian Americans. However, based on current statistical projections, they are expected to become the largest Asian American group in the future.

Holidays and Celebrations

Christmas: Christmas has been the longest and best-loved festivity among Filipinos. Preparatory to the celebration, a novena is started on Dec. 16, known as *Misas de Aguinaldo*, or Gift Mass. *Misas de Aguinaldo* started in Mexico in 1587, when Fray Diego de Soria, prior of the convent of San Agustin Acolman, petitioned the Pope for permission to hold Christmastide Masses outdoors because the church could not accommodate the multitude that attended the services. The request that granted these Masses came to be known as *Misas de Aguinaldo.*

Philippine Independence Day—June 12: On June 12, Filipino Americans all over the United States celebrate Philippine Independence Day. This festival features parades, folk dances, food and craft fairs, music and other forms of cultural performances. This is a time of pride to remember and celebrate their culture and heritage.

Rizal Day—Dec. 30: Filipino Americans also observe Rizal Day on Dec. 30 to commemorate the martyrdom of their national hero, Jose Rizal. He gave his life to fighting for the Philippines Independence from Spain.

<u>Filipino-American Friendship Day—July 4</u>: Filipino-American Friendship Day commemorates July 4, 1946, when the United States granted the Philippines independence.

NOTES

Japanese Americans

Japanese Americans
SUMMARY

Demographics

- The Japanese American population is not as large as it once was. There are now approximately 833,761 Japanese Americans in the United States, down 1.63 percent from their 1990 total of 847,562.
- The most Japanese-populated state is California, followed by Hawaii. The biggest Japanese market is Los Angeles County, followed by Honolulu County.

Cultural Insights

- The bow is the traditional Japanese greeting. If someone bows to greet you, observe him or her carefully. Bow to the same depth as you have been bowed to, because the depth of the bow indicates the status relationship between you. As you bow, lower your eyes. Keep your palms flat against your thighs.
- Unacculturated Japanese can experience a great deal of anxiety about life because of the need to save face. There are constant pressures to conform. A strong work ethic and strong group relationships give structure and stability to life. Emotional restraints are developed in early childhood.
- The most important holiday among Japanese Americans is New Year's Day.

Business Practices: Dos and Don'ts

Dos

- Be punctual at all times.
- A personal call is better than a letter. A letter might not even be answered.
- When meeting the client for the first time, make sure to exchange business cards.
- The proper way to accept a business card is with the index finger and thumb of both hands and by acknowledging with a nod that you have absorbed the information on it.
- Because age equals rank, show the greatest respect to the oldest members of the Japanese group with whom you are in contact.

Don'ts

- Don't make accusations or refuse anything directly; be indirect. Also, don't ask questions that your counterpart might be unable to answer.
- As a general rule of thumb, the Japanese tend to be quite serious on the job.
- Don't bow to greet a Japanese individual before he or she bows to you. They might be acculturated and feel slighted by your assumption.

Japanese Americans

Demographics

The Japanese American community is the only major Asian subgroup that has shown a decline in size of the population. There are now approximately 833,761 Japanese Americans in the United States, down 1.63 percent from their 1990 total of 847,562. The population decreased by almost 13,801 people and fell from being the third-largest Asian group in 1990 down to sixth place in the 2005 Census American Community Survey count.

The 10 most Japanese populated states in 2005 were:

1. California (311,559)
2. Hawaii (200,893)
3. Washington (40,115)
4. New York (33,864)
5. Illinois (20,672)
6. Texas (19,386)
7. Michigan (15,186)
8. Florida (14,624)
9. New Jersey (14,131)
10. Virginia (13,865)

The top eight Japanese markets by county in the United States in 2005 were:

1. Los Angeles County (297,345)
2. Honolulu County (161,568)
3. King County (Seattle) (26,031)
4. San Diego County (20,064)
5. Cook County (Chicago) (13,729)
6. Sacramento County CA (13,391)
7. San Francisco County (12,255)
8. New York County (10,954)

Cultural Insights

Worldview

- Hierarchy and formality are valued in Japanese culture.

- The Japanese have a great respect for authority and tradition.

Sense of Self

- Japanese Americans are more acculturated than other Asian American populations. Younger generation Japanese Americans think and behave more in line with traditional Western values. Thus, they are known to think and behave more independently than older, less acculturated Japanese.

Sense of Space

- Japanese Americans tend to require more personal space than the general population.

Communication Style

- The Japanese are often indirect in their communication style. For example, a Japanese response of, "I'll consider it," might actually mean, "No." A "Yes," (*hai*) might mean, "I agree," "I understand," or "I am agreeing in order to avoid causing embarrassment and loss of face."

Unacculturated Japanese are more comfortable with long silences than are traditional members of the general market.

- In negotiating, if there is a problem or a conflicting opinion, the Japanese will not refute it directly. They will not summarize, finalize or give a direct complaint regarding the issue in question.

- The bow is the traditional Japanese greeting. If someone bows to greet you, observe carefully. The depth of the bow indicates the status of the relationship between you. If you want to demonstrate respect, bow lower than the other person. This is always the case when dealing with a boss or superior. Unacculturated Japanese women always bow lower than men. As you bow, lower your eyes. Keep your palms flat against the front of your thighs. Women can either bow with their palms against their thighs or in the fig leaf position. Another way to indicate respect is to be the last to finish the bow. Since there is a high degree of acculturation and assimilation among Japanese, be cautious about when you bow. A good rule of thumb is to watch your client. If he/she bows first, respond in kind.

Eye Contact

- Direct eye contact is not the norm among older generation Japanese. They feel that it is rude to look directly into someone else's eyes.

- Younger generation Japanese feel that having eye contact is important during conversation. It shows sincerity.

Language

- Japanese is the official language of Japan. It is a complex and subtle language, and is spoken nowhere else in the world as a primary tongue. Most sentences in Japanese can be expressed on at least four different levels of politeness. Japanese women almost always use one of the more deferential forms. Communication in Japan is often marked by great subtlety; information is left unspoken, yet it is perfectly understood.

- Many Japanese use the polite form when speaking about themselves and the honorific form when speaking about someone else. The entire language is geared toward giving respect to the other party by lowering the speaker's/writer's own status.

- The 2005 Census data shows that 45.1 percent of Japanese Americans speak a language well. The number of Japanese reporting that they speak English only was 54.9 percent.

Time and Time Consciousness

- Be punctual at all times. The Japanese value time and are conscious about spending their time wisely.

Values and Norms

- Like other immigrant groups, the *Issei* (first generation) had a strong, lasting commitment to education. Most viewed education as a way out of the low-wage jobs on the farms and in nurseries where they worked and as a route to better-paying positions.

- In Japanese culture, hard work is looked upon as a desirable goal in itself. It plays a prominent part in their socialization and is reinforced in their contacts with American culture.

- Japanese culture stresses the importance of harmony and the need to save face. Saving face means avoiding causing or being the object of embarrassment and shame. There are constant pressures to conform. A strong work ethic and emphasis on the well-being of the group give structure and stability to life. Emotional restraints are developed in childhood. For many unacculturated Japanese, this repression of emotion might result in the experience of anxiety.

Business Practices: Dos and Don'ts

Dos

- Be punctual at all times.

- A personal call is better than a letter. A letter might not even be answered.

- When meeting the client for the first time, make sure to exchange business cards.

- The proper way to accept a business card is with the index finger and thumb of both hands and to acknowledge with a nod that you have absorbed the information on it. Do not write on the card or put it away without carefully reading it.

- Because age equals rank, show the greatest respect to the oldest members of the Japanese group with whom you are in contact.

- Japanese culture is quite formal, and the Japanese value appropriate mannerly behavior. One place you can demonstrate your respect for this culture is when eating. For example, women or men who are perceived to have less status usually pour drinks (tea, coffee, beer, sake) for those who have more status. Typically, an individual will not pour his/her own beverages. If someone offers to pour a beverage for you, accept graciously. Among older generations, it is important to hold the cup with both hands and bow a nod of thanks.

Don'ts

* Don't make accusations or refuse anything directly, be indirect. Also, don't ask questions that your counterpart might be unable to answer.

* On the job, the Japanese tend to be quite serious and do not try to lighten things up with humor.

* When splitting wooden chopsticks, never rub them together to smooth a rough surface. It is considered impolite to leave chopsticks on your plate or on the food. When you are speaking or finished with your meal, place the chopsticks on a chopstick holder (small dish or plate or paper on the table). Never stab your food with chopsticks (e.g., a bowl of rice). This can be considered highly offensive and an omen of death. Also, never gesture with your chopsticks. When speaking, put them down.

Historical Background

Japan can be said to have taken its first steps to nationhood in the Yamato period, which began at the end of the third century A.D. During this period, the ancestors of the present emperor began to unify small independent states to form them into a nation.

In 604, Prince Shotoku laid down Japan's first constitution. At this time, Buddhism, which had been introduced from the Eurasian continent, began to take root in Japan. The Nara period began at the beginning of the eighth century with the establishment of the country's first permanent capital in Nara. Toward the end of the century, the capital was transferred to Kyoto, launching the Heian period, during which noble families predominated and a distinct national culture blossomed.

From the Kamakura period, which began at the end of the 12th century, to the close of the Edo period in the latter half of the 19th century, the *samurai*, or warrior class, ruled Japan. Order broke down around the middle of the 15th century, and Japan was torn by civil warfare for nearly 100 years as *samurai* lords of different domains fought one another. The agent of pacification and national unity was Toyotomi Hideyoshi.

At the beginning of the 17th century, Tokugawa Ieyasu set up a government in Edo (now Tokyo), and the Edo period began. The Tokugawa regime adopted an isolationist policy that lasted for more than 200 years, cutting off exchange with all countries except China and the Netherlands. But with the arrival of American Commodore Matthew Perry in 1853, the nation began to open itself up to the United States and European powers.

The age of the *samurai* came to an end with the Meiji Restoration of 1868, and a new system of government centered on the emperor was established. The new government promoted modernization; adopted Western political, social and economic systems; and stimulated industrial activity. The Diet (legislature) was inaugurated and the people began to have limited participation in politics.

Circa 1920, a democratic movement gained strength. But amid a global economic crisis, the military came to the fore, and Japan eventually marched down the road to war. The Japanese were colonizing and oppressing much of Asia when the United States cut off its supply of oil and other goods and resources. Subsequently, the Japanese attacked Pearl Harbor.

At the outbreak of World War II, the Japanese citizens (*Issei*, first generation) and their Japanese American children residing in the United States were ordered by the U.S. government into wartime detention camps. As prisoners of war for up to five years, they left behind homes, farms, businesses and personal property, without any promise of return and often for good. Still, thousands of young Japanese American men enlisted and served in the Army's 442nd Regiment and 100th Battalion, all while their families were imprisoned. These were the most decorated units in the U.S. Army. With the end of the war, the veterans returned home and reunited with their families. Many would continue to serve their country and communities as politicians, businessmen and physicians.

With the end of World War II in 1945, Japan had newfound respect for the United States and a new constitution. Japan was committed to becoming a peace-seeking democracy and to succeed in relaunching their economy. In 1956, the nation's entry into the United Nations was approved. Since then, Japan has contributed to world peace and prosperity as a member of the international community.

Immigration to the United States

In the 1870s and 1880s, the Hawaiian sugar industry boomed. This stood in sharp contrast to Japan's painful transition to a modern economy that produced large-scale unemployment, bankruptcies and civil disorders. These factors contributed to a large portion of Japanese emigrants moving to Hawaii. Thus, as of 1900, the majority of all the Japanese immigrants living in the United States lived in the Hawaiian islands. From 1885 through 1894, more than 28,000 Japanese migrated to Hawaii, the vast majority of them single men.

Japanese relations with U.S. society were to some extent shaped by the fact that they followed in the wake of the Chinese. Both in Hawaii and on the mainland, the Chinese had started as laborers and many had worked their way up to become small-business owners. They were resented and rejected for their advancement and competition. The Japanese began in the same fashion and were initially welcomed as substitutes for the Chinese as coolie labor. Their rising advancement and success, however, soon lumped them together with the Chinese as the "Yellow Peril" that threatened the living standard of American workers and businessmen and American society in general.

On Dec. 7, 1941, Japan's attack on Pearl Harbor set the stage for a traumatic landmark in the history of Japanese Americans. In retaliation for the attack, which occurred in the midst of negotiations seemingly aimed at peace, anti-Japanese sentiment ran high. As a result, Japanese Americans were interned in concentration camps and lost their property without any due process of law. The rationalization was used that they were a threat for sabotage and espionage. However, research has shown that there were no documented cases of Japanese Americans being involved in espionage or sabotage for Japan. Japanese Americans were among the most decorated of any citizens who fought for the United States in World War II.

The economic effects of wartime internment were reflected in the postwar occupational decline among Japanese Americans. The number of first-generation Japanese business owners dropped to half of what it had been in prewar years, with the number of domestic servants of the same generation more than doubling. Those who became farm laborers in the postwar years were more than triple the prewar percentage, and the number of Japanese professionals also declined. But while disastrous economic retrogression struck the first-generation Japanese Americans (*Issei*), the second generation (*Nisei*) steamed along at an accelerated rate. The 2000 Census showed the median family income of Japanese Americans to be 45 percent higher than that of native-born, non-Asian Americans. Along with this economic progress came acculturation and social acceptance, including rising rates of intermarriage.

Religion

Japanese immigrants brought Buddhism and Shintoism with them when they first came to the United States. However, once they arrived Protestant missionaries converted many to Christian beliefs. By the 1920s, there were thousands of practicing Japanese American Protestants. The church has become an important institution of and means for maintaining the Japanese American community.

Degree of Acculturation

Successful adaptation to the larger U.S. society consists mainly in acculturation, measured by the ability of a group to share and follow the values, goals and expected behaviors of the majority. By this criteria, the Japanese Americans have been quite successful. Japanese Americans values, skills, attitudes and behaviors do not differ from those of the average American.

The Japanese American Market

Japanese Americans are often considered the most assimilated segment of the Asian American population, because they comprise the only group with a significant number of second- and third-generation members. Furthermore, Japanese Americans have the highest percentage of marriage outside their ethnic group of any Asian population living in the United States. The Japanese American market is complex and can be divided into four groups: assimilated, *Shinisse* (new immigrants), students and expatriate business transfers.

Holidays and Celebrations

New Year's Day (*Shogatsu*)—Jan. 1: New Year's Day is one of the most important holidays on the Japanese calendar. The holiday is often celebrated for several days before and after Jan. 1.

Girls Day (*Hinamatsuri*)—March 3: On Girls Day, some Japanese families with daughters will pray for their health and happiness. Traditionally, families will display *hina ningyou* (dolls especially made for this festival), offer *hishi mochi* (red, white and green rice cakes) and peach blossoms, and drink *shiro zake* (a sweet sake).

Children's Day (*Kodomo no Hi*)—May 5: Children's Day is one of the most popularly celebrated national holidays in Japan. Traditionally known as the Boys Festival or *tango ni sekku* (Iris Festival), families with boys celebrate it and pray for the health and happiness of their boys. Traditionally, families hang *koinobori* (cloth streamers in the shape of carp) from balconies and display *gogatsu ningyo* (samurai dolls) indoors. Children take a special bath called *syobuyu* (a bath with floating iris leaves) and eat *kashiwi mochi* (a rice cake wrapped in a lotus leaf) and *chimaki* (a dumpling wrapped in bamboo leaves).

Nisei-Week Festival: This is an event that is celebrated annually by Japanese Americans in Los Angeles in mid-August. Its mission is to celebrate and share Japanese and Japanese American history and culture while revitalizing commerce in L.A.'s Little Tokyo community.

Respect for the Aged Day (*Keiro no Hi*)—Sept. 15: Sept. 15 is a national holiday in Japan that honors the elderly and celebrates their longevity. It is a relatively new holiday, so there are no customs particularly associated with the day.

NOTES

Jewish Americans

Jewish Americans
SUMMARY

Demographics
- There are over 6,00,000 Jews in the United States.
- The most Jewish populated states are New York, California and Florida.
- The most Jewish populated cities are New York City, Los Angeles and Chicago.

Cultural Insights
- Jewish identity is largely based on one's place in the family and community, as well as on individual achievement.
- For many, practicing the Jewish faith is central to their identity. Most Jews, however, are not strictly religious.
- Jews place a high value on education and educational achievement.
- Traditionally, observant Jews pray three times a day and follow traditional religious guidelines for daily life strictly, including kosher dietary practices and rules regarding the appropriate behavior of men and women in their community.
- Many Jews identify strongly with what happens in Israel. Although they are first and foremost Americans, they have a strong spiritual and emotional connection to Israel.
- Passover, Shavuot, Sukkot, Rosh Hashanah and Yom Kippur are the five most important festivals of the Jewish year. Hanukkah and Purim, though widely observed, are less important.

Business Practices: Dos and Don'ts

Dos

- Remember that the Jewish Sabbath begins at sundown on Friday and ends Saturday evening. Observant Jews conduct no business on Friday evenings or on Saturdays.
- Remember the Jewish holidays, especially Rosh Hashanah, Passover and Yom Kippur. Do not schedule appointments during these times.
- Among Orthodox Jews, attire should be modest.
- Expect business to be straightforward.

Don'ts

- Some observant Orthodox Jews cannot shake hands with members of the opposite sex who are outside of their immediate family. For a woman, the best policy is to refrain from offering to shake hands; she should wait for her counterparts to initiate this gesture.

Jewish Americans

Demographics

There are over 6,000,000 Jews in the United States.

The 10 most Jewish populated states are:

1. New York (1,651,000)
2. California (967,000)
3. Florida (637,000)
4. New Jersey (465,000)
5. Pennsylvania (282,000)
6. Massachusetts (274,000)
7. Illinois (270,000)
8. Maryland (216,000)
9. Ohio (144,000
10. Texas (124,000)

The most Jewish populated cities are:

1. New York City (1,750,000)
2. Miami (535,000)
3. Los Angeles (490,000)
4. Philadelphia (254,000)
5. Chicago (248,000)
6. San Francisco (210,000)
7. Boston (208,000)
8. Washington, D.C. (165,000)

Cultural Insights

Worldview

- The Jewish worldview is rooted in a history of struggle, perseverance and rebirth.

- The Holocaust and Israel are closely linked in the perceptions of most contemporary Jews as symbols of collective death and rebirth. For many, Israel has an important symbolic significance, embodying Jewish self-respect and the promise of fulfillment.

Sense of Self

- Jewish identity is largely based on one's heritage, religious identification, personal expression and place in the community, as well as individual and group achievement.

  Unlike most other White ethnic groups, Jews largely base their identity in their heritage and religion.

Sense of Space

- As with other ethnic groups, some Jews might speak at a much closer distance than is customary among mainstream Americans. Some observant Jews avoid any physical contact with any members of the opposite sex outside the immediate family. Please note that not all Orthodox Jews avoid this type of contact. In this regard, however, it is best to be conservative and adjust your behavior and actions to the situation.

Communication Style

- An all-purpose greeting in Hebrew is *shalom*, used for both "hello" and "good-bye". It also means "peace". However, this greeting is not typically used. If you attend a religious celebration, like a wedding or a bar mitzvah or bat mitzvah, it is traditional to wish the family *mazel tov* (good luck).

- A traditional sentiment for a Rosh Hashanah (the Jewish New Year) is, "May you have a happy and a sweet new year (*Shana Tova*)".

Eye Contact

- In observant Orthodox communities, men refrain from looking any woman in the eyes unless she is his wife or daughter.

Language

- Hebrew is one of the world's oldest languages and is the national language of Israel. There are 4.5 million Hebrew speakers in Israel and more than 100,000 in the United States. After Hebrew's initial decline around 200 A.D., it ceased to be widely spoken as a language by the ninth century. It was reborn as a modern language in the 19th century. The Hebrew alphabet of 22 letters consists entirely of consonants. The language is written from right to left without vowels. Around the eighth century, a system developed for indicating vowels through the use of small dots and dashes placed above and below the consonants.

- Yiddish is a language developed among Jews living in Eastern Europe. Its basic structure is a medieval form of German, with many words borrowed from Hebrew and a few other languages. To the untrained eye, written Yiddish looks identical to Hebrew because it is written from right to left and with the Hebrew alphabet. It differs, however, in that it does not use the system of dots and dashes below the letters.

- Jews in the United States speak English. Hebrew is mostly for use in religious ceremonies and cultural practices. Jewish organizations often provide English-speaking classes for newly arrived immigrants. Many older European Jews—and, to a lesser extent, their American-born children—speak Yiddish

Time and Time Consciousness

- Often people are less rigid about time in Jewish communities than in mainstream America. This can be especially true for social occasions. As regards professional and business appointments, however, punctuality is expected.

Values and Norms

- Most Jews are not strictly religious, although practicing the Jewish faith is central to the identity of many. Many Jews who do not identify religiously resonate to a cultural identity, wrapped up in their socialization, customs, rituals and history.

- Jews place a high value on education and educational achievement. A higher percentage of Jews attend colleges and universities than mainstream Americans.

- Family is extremely important in Jewish communities, and deference is often given to elders.

- Central to Jewish cultural and religious survival in the United States has been the priority placed on community, community organization and mutual support.

- Besides their focus on community, the Jewish population also is known to stress the importance of individual achievement and success.

Religious/Cultural Practices and Beliefs

- There are four organized forms of Judaism in the United States: Orthodox, Conservative, Reform and Reconstructionist. Approximately 7 percent of practicing Jews in the United States are Orthodox, 35 percent are Conservative, 43 percent are Reform and 1 percent are Reconstructionist (for more information on Jewish movements, please read "The Jewish American" below).

- It is important to understand that Jewish holidays are typically considered Holy Days by the observant. That is to say, they are more reverential, serious and religious in nature than what is typically considered to be a holiday.

- Traditionally, observant Jews (mostly Orthodox and some Conservative) pray three times a day: in the morning (*shaharith*), afternoon (*minchah*) and evening (*maariv*).

- As a sign of devotion to God, the observant adult male Jew wears both a fringed prayer shawl (a *tallith*, the fringes of which are called *zizith*) and phylacteries (prayer boxes, called *tefillin*) containing slips inscribed with scriptural passages used during weekday morning prayers. One set of phylacteries is worn on the left arm and one set is worn on the head.

- Many will place a *mezuzah* (prayer box) on the doorpost of their home. A *mezuzah* is a small, rectangle-shaped, hollow object which contains an important prayer. As a gesture of respect to God, the head is covered during prayer, either with a hat or a skullcap (a *kippah,* or in Yiddish, a *yarmulke*). Pious Jews wear a head covering at all times. Many also will wear a small *tallith* under their shirts with only the fringes showing.

- More observant Jews will follow kosher dietary practices. Certain animals, considered unclean, are not to be eaten. Into this category fall pigs, as well as fish without fins and scales. Edible animals include those that have split hooves and chew their cuds.

Animals must be properly slaughtered and the blood fully drained before the meat can be eaten. Meat and milk products are not to be eaten together.

- A minority of Orthodox Jews will follow the biblical commandment that men do not "take a razor" to "the corners of their beards". Modern Orthodox do shave. Hassidic Jews (a group of highly observant Orthodox Jews who emphasize piety and joyous worship) do not shave at all. Some trim their beards but leave the *payos* (earlocks) alone.

- A minority of Orthodox married women may not show their hair to men outside their immediate family. Thus, they will wear a combination of wigs, kerchiefs and hats.

- At Sabbath and holiday services, one of the key components is reading from one of the five books of Moses (The Torah) and a coincident reading from the Prophets (The Haftorah). The Torah is hand-written on special scroll and is kept in the ark usually found on the pulpit.

Business Practices: Dos and Don'ts

Dos

- Remember the Jewish Sabbath, which begins on Friday at sunset and ends on Saturday at dark. It is meant to be a day of rest and relaxation. During this time, religious Jews do not work, drive, carry anything outside their residence, conduct business affairs, touch or spend money, answer telephones, watch television or use computers. They are also prohibited from asking a non-Jew to do so for them. More observant Jews might close their businesses early on Fridays. No business is conducted on Saturdays.

- Remember Jewish holidays, especially Rosh Hashanah and Yom Kippur (the High Holy Days). Do not schedule appointments during these times. It is allowable to schedule appointments during the intermediate days of Passover (avoid scheduling appointments during the first two or last two days of the holiday). On Passover, observant Jews have additional prohibitions to their diet, which include not eating anything with leavening.

- Among Orthodox Jews, attire should be modest. Garments should have sleeves, and dress length should be below the knee. Among some groups, men and women should not wear shorts, and women should not wear trousers. Men and married women might be required to have their heads covered.

- Expect business to be straightforward.

- A traditional Orthodox Jewish male might not always introduce his wife. If this is the case, let it pass without comment and do not try to draw her into the conversation.

- Most Jews in America are not strictly observant of kosher dietary practices (other than possibly avoiding shellfish, pork and pork byproducts). On the other hand, more observant Jews might avoid food and drink with additives, gelling agents, and colorings that contain prohibited ingredients. If in doubt, ask if business associates/customers are strictly kosher.

Don'ts

- Some observant Orthodox Jews, (the men are usually distinguished by their skullcaps or hats), cannot shake hands with members of the opposite sex who are outside their immediate family. Don't be offended.

- For a woman, the best policy is to refrain from offering to shake hands; she should wait for her counterparts to initiate this gesture.

Historical/Religious Background

Judaism is one of the world's oldest continuing religions. It originated in the land of Israel (also known as Palestine) in the Middle East. While Judaism has changed forms over time, some characteristics have remained the same. One is its strict monotheism. God revealed himself to the Israelites at Mount Sinai, and the Torah ("revealed instruction") is God's will expressed in 613 commandments (*mizvoth*), with which individuals are to regulate their entire lives. There are two parts of the Torah: the written Torah and the oral Torah. The written Torah (*Tenach*) contains the Five Books of Moses (*Chumashe Torah*), the Prophets (*Nevi'im*), and Writings (*Ketuvim*). The oral Torah, explanations of the written Torah, was originally passed down verbally from generation to generation and was maintained by rabbis (teachers). Eventually, it was decided that the oral Torah should be written down. In the second century, the *Mishnah* (an outline of the oral Torah) was developed. Discussions of the Mishnah by Jewish scholars became known as the *Gemara*. The combination of the *Mishnah* and the *Gemara* is the Talmud.

Another major aspect of Judaism is the covenant (*berith*) between God and the Jewish people. In return for acknowledging God as their ultimate king and obeying His laws, God would acknowledge Israel as His people and be especially mindful of them. At the same time, the covenant establishes that Israel's well-being depends on obedience to God's commandments.

For the traditionally observant, a third aspect of Judaism is the belief that the Messiah (*Mashiach*) will be a person (not a god) from the family of King David who will lead the world to unity and peace. Jews do not believe that Jesus was the Messiah.

The Jewish Diaspora

As a result of both forced exile and voluntary migrations, Jewish communities have existed at one time or another in almost all parts of the world. In the early 1990s, the total world Jewish population was about 12.8 million, of whom about 45 percent lived in the United States, 30 percent in Israel, and 9 percent in the Soviet Union. The remainder is spread throughout the world.

Immigration to the United States

Jews were said to have been among the explorers and settlers who first settled the New World. They were fleeing persecution in Europe. The first officially recorded Jews came to the area that would become the United States in the 1650s from Spain, Portugal and the Netherlands as refugees from the Spanish Inquisition. The first significant group of Jewish immigrants, however, largely came from Germany in the 1850s. These mostly male immigrants often began working as tradesmen, but quickly built businesses and were absorbed into the middle class.

The majority of Jews in the United States today are descendents of Eastern European immigrants who arrived between 1880 and 1924. During this period, more than 2 million immigrants from Poland and Russia came to this country fleeing extreme, government-sanctioned persecution (including murderous race riots called *pogroms*). The majority of these immigrants were merchants, shopkeepers and craftsmen and, unlike the former group, came as entire families. These immigrants brought with them a rich Yiddish culture and were more likely to form and maintain cohesive communities than the Germans, who often considered themselves more "American" than these later arrivals.

Between the late 1930s and 1945, approximately 6 million European Jews (1 million of whom were children) were exterminated by Nazi Germany in the genocide known as the Holocaust. During this time, thousands of homeless European Jews entered the United States. Since then, Jews from other areas of the world, including Iran and Syria, have enriched American Jewish communities. Since the collapse of the Soviet Union, there has been another influx of Russian Jews. Unlike earlier Russian immigrants, these Soviet Jews had scant opportunity to maintain Jewish rituals and customs or to study Hebrew in their native land.

Jews in the United States have a strong emotional and spiritual bond with the state of Israel and are concerned about its stability and well-being.

Jewish immigrants to the United States faced various forms of discrimination. Aside from very common anti-Semitic campaigns, many Jews have had socialist views. This has exposed many of them to antileftist campaigns. From the time of their arrival until the 1960s, discriminatory policies prohibited Jews from joining social and athletic clubs, visiting resort hotels and living in certain neighborhoods. When Jewish attendance in private northeastern colleges and universities began to approach that of mainstream Whites in the 1920s, many of these institutions established quotas to limit the number of Jewish students admitted, regardless of their qualifications. In the early 1950s, 20 percent of all job openings in Los Angeles and Chicago requested non-Jewish applicants. Until the late 1960s, few Jews could find employment in large law firms or major industrial corporations, one factor that explains their high levels of self-employment.

Although negative stereotypes and attitudes toward Jews continue among some groups, blatant and legalized anti-Semitism decreased sharply when North Americans were confronted by the horrors of the Holocaust during WWII and the Civil Rights Movement of the 1960s.

Today, Jewish Americans have risen to high levels of accomplishment in all areas of social, economic and political life. Work ethic and values that stress family, education and community organization have heavily influenced Jewish success. However, most studies agree that their high levels of education upon arrival, combined with the growing economy in the Northeast in the early 20th century, also played major roles.

The Jewish American Market

Most Jews in the United States are descendents of Ashkenazi Jews, those from Central and Eastern Europe. There is also a small number of descendents of Sephardic Jews, those primarily from southern Spain, Persia and the Middle East. Some Sephardic Jews are culturally indistinguishable from others in the Jewish community. However, some Sephardin are quite connected with their Middle Eastern cultural roots.

There are basically three forms of Judaism in the United States: Reform, Conservative, and Orthodox. Reform Judaism was the first movement to officially establish itself and was largely German in its beginning. It has been heavily influenced by liberal Protestantism. Since the 1940s, it has put significant emphasis on Jewish peoplehood and traditional religious culture with much less emphasis on traditional religious practice and law. Its orientation is liberal and non-authoritarian. The Conservative movement was largely established by Eastern European Jews. It respects traditional Jewish law and practice, while advocating a flexible approach to *Halakah* (a body of traditional law). Community and piety are important to Conservative Jews. An offshoot of this movement is the Reconstructionist movement founded in the 1930s, which combines a strong commitment to tradition with the search for contemporary meaning. It also places a strong emphasis on Jewish peoplehood and culture. Orthodox Jews represent a spectrum of traditionalist groups, ranging from the Modern Orthodox, who try to integrate traditional observance with modern life, to some Hasidic sects that do not have a contemporary focus and attempt to shut out the modern world.

There are significant cultural differences between the groups, primarily between the highly Orthodox and the others. Many Orthodox (here and in Israel) do not consider the non-Orthodox to be truly Jewish. This subject has caused a great deal of pain and anguish in the Jewish community, especially since the assassination of Yitzhak Rabin by another Jew.

Another topic for debate within the Jewish community is whether Judaism is a race or a religion. While there have been genetic studies that have found genes specific to Jews, one can also convert to Judaism. There are people, therefore, who claim to be Jewish even though they do not believe in the basic principles of the religion, and there are those who claim to be Jewish solely because they practice Judaism.

Degree of Acculturation

Community has always been important among Jewish Americans. For example, Jews have developed institutions like B'nai B'rith to provide for community needs. They also have founded schools and universities where the focus is maintaining Jewish tradition, faith and culture. Many synagogues have Hebrew schools where young Jewish children go two or three times a week to learn Jewish tradition and the Hebrew language. Since the founding of Israel in 1948, efforts to aid Israel have provided a major focus for the Jewish American community.

Jewish Americans are constantly facing the pressures of assimilation into mainstream American culture. Thus, religious and institutional involvement among Jewish Americans has steadily declined. Jews are more likely than any other White ethnic group to marry co-ethnics. However, an increasing number (more than 50 percent) are marrying non-Jews. Despite their rapid assimilation into mainstream American society, Jewish Americans maintain many elements particular to their culture. When compared to other White ethnics, Jews tend to live near other members of their group. Jews also tend to retain the liberal politics and Democratic Party affiliations generally associated with the working class.

Economic Status

Despite their experience with discrimination, Jewish Americans have risen to high levels of accomplishment in all areas of social, economic and political life. More than 80 percent of college-age Jewish Americans attend institutions of higher learning, a proportion twice that of the population at large. Jews are well represented in high-income professions requiring a college education, such as medicine, law, engineering and accounting, and have high rates of self-employment.

Holidays and Celebrations

The Jewish day begins and ends at sunset. Therefore, all holidays begin at sundown on the evening before the date listed. Also, the Jewish calendar is primarily lunar-based, so dates will change every year. Passover, *Shavuot*, *Sukkot*, *Rosh Hashanah* and *Yom Kippur* are the five most important festivals of the Jewish year. *Hanukkah* and *Purim*, though popular and widely celebrated, are less important.

Sabbath (*Shabbat*): *Shabbat*, the Jewish Sabbath, is at the end of the workweek. *Shabbat* is meant to commemorate the period of time in which God rested after creating the world. *Shabbat* is designated as a day of rest when work is prohibited. It commences at sundown on Friday night with the lighting of candles, a *kiddush* (blessing recited over wine), a *hamotzi* (blessing recited over bread) and the chanting of psalms of praise to God. On Friday evening, the bread that is traditionally eaten is a braided loaf of egg bread called a *challah*. The next morning, *Shabbat* services begin around 9 a.m. and continue until about noon. After services, the family might have a leisurely meal. *Shabbat* ends at nightfall, approximately 40 minutes after sunset.

Rosh Hashanah: *Rosh Hashanah* is the Jewish New Year. It is a celebration of the world's creation and a day of self-examination, repentance and divine judgment. The start of *Rosh Hashanah* begins with a candle blessing, a *kiddush* (a blessing recited over wine), a *hamotzi* (a blessing recited over bread) and a special meal. The *challah* that is traditionally served for the High Holy Days is a round loaf. People attend services at their local synagogue and do not usually attend work or school. The Orthodox and many Conservative Jews traditionally observe two days of Rosh Hashanah. Reform and some Conservative Jews observe one day.

Yom Kippur: Ten days after the start of *Rosh Hashanah* is *Yom Kippur*, or the "Day of Atonement". *Yom Kippur* is a day of fasting and praying. There are five Prohibitions of *Yom Kippur*: no eating or drinking, no wearing perfumes or lotions, no sexual relations, no washing, and no wearing of leather shoes. *Yom Kippur* and *Rosh Hashanah* are known as the High Holy Days.

Sukkot: Sukkot is a harvest festival that lasts for seven days. It also commemorates the Hebrews' 40 years of wandering in the desert. Orthodox and observant Conservative Jews do not work on the first and last days. Observant Reform Jews might attend services on the first day of this festival.

Shemini Atzeret: *Shemini Atzeret* means "the eighth day of assembly", and it follows *Sukkot*.

Simchat Torah: *Simchat Torah* is the second day of *Shemini Atzeret*. This day celebrates the reading of the last chapter of the Torah.

Chanukah (Hanukkah): Hanukkah is a celebration of Jewish national survival and religious freedom. It celebrates the Maccabees victory over the Greco-Syrians and the rededication of the Holy Temple of Jerusalem. The lighting of Hanukkah candles is in remembrance of a miracle. After the temple was rededicated, there was only enough consecrated oil available to burn for one day. This little bit of oil lasted for eight days, until more could be prepared.

The lighting of the candles is the most important Hanukkah custom. Other Hanukkah customs include eating fried potato pancakes and playing a game with a small top that has Hebrew letters on its sides (a *dreidel*). Because Hanukkah falls around the same time as Christmas, many Jews also give gifts during that period. Working is permitted during this holiday.

Purim: American Jews sometimes refer to *Purim* as the Jewish Mardi Gras. The day celebrates the time when Esther, a beautiful young Jewish woman, saved the Jews from annihilation in Persia. Jews are told to eat, drink and be merry on this day, as well as to send out gifts of food or drink, and to make gifts to charity. Children, and sometimes adults, might come to synagogue in costumes. It is customary to make noise whenever the name Haman (the King's evil adviser who plotted to annihilate the Jews of Persia) is mentioned. Working is allowed on this day.

Passover: The primary observances of Passover are related to the Exodus from Egypt after 400 years of slavery. The name Passover refers to the fact that God "passed over" the houses of the Jews when he was slaying the firstborn of Egypt. One of the most significant observances of the holiday is not eating *chametz* (leaven). *Chametz* includes anything made from the five major grains (wheat, rye, barley, oats and spelt). This commemorates the fact that the Jews leaving Egypt were in a hurry and did not have time to let their bread rise. The grain product eaten during Passover is called *matzah*. *Matzah* is unleavened bread, made simply from flour and water and cooked very quickly. Another significant observance is the *Seder* meal, usually held the first two evenings of the holiday. *Seder* means "order" in Hebrew. This meal is full of ritual and pageantry that recounts the Jewish people's deliverance from slavery. Passover lasts for seven days. For the Orthodox and observant Conservative Jews, the first two and last two days of the holiday are days on which no work is permitted. Those Reform Jews who are observant might attend services on the first day of the holiday. Agriculturally, Passover represents the beginning of the harvest season in Israel, but little attention is paid to this aspect of the holiday.

Holocaust Remembrance Day (*Yom Ha-Shoah*): This is a memorial day for those who died in the Holocaust.

Israel's Independence Day (*Yom Ha-Atzmaut*): This day marks the establishment of the modern state of Israel in 1948.

Shavuot: Agriculturally, this holiday commemorates the time when the first fruits were harvested and brought to the ancient temple as a sacrifice. Historically, this holy day celebrates the giving of the Torah at Mount Sinai. For the Orthodox and observant Conservative Jews, work is not permitted during *Shavuot*. Observant Reform Jews might attend services on this holiday.

Ninth of Av (*Tisha B-Av*): *Tisha B'Av*, or the Fast of the Ninth of Av (a Jewish month), is a day of mourning to commemorate the tragedies that have befallen the Jewish people, many of which coincidentally have occurred on the ninth of Av. The restrictions on *Tisha B'Av* are similar to those on Yom Kippur: to refrain from eating and drinking (even water); washing, bathing, shaving or wearing cosmetics; wearing leather shoes; and engaging in sexual relations. Work is also restricted.

Life Cycle Events

Circumcision (*berith milah* or *bris*): At the age of eight days, a male child is publicly initiated into the covenant of Abraham through circumcision.

Bar Mitzvah: Boys reach religious maturity at the age of 13, when they assume responsibility for observing all the commandments (*bar mitzvah*) and are called for the first time to read from the Torah in synagogue.

Bat Mitzvah: Girls also reach religious maturity at 13 years of age and, in modern liberal synagogues, also read from the Torah.

Confirmation: In the 19th century, the modernizing Reform movement instituted the practice of confirmation for both young men and women of secondary school age. The ceremony is held on Shavuot and signifies acceptance of the faith revealed at Sinai.

Marriage: The next turning point in a Jew's life is marriage (*kiddushin*, or "sanctification"). The seven wedding benedictions include prayers for the rebuilding of Jerusalem and the return of the Jewish people to Zion. The wedding takes place under a canopy. It ends when the groom stomps on a glass and the guests shout "*Mazel tov.*"

Death: At the Jewish funeral, the hope for resurrection of the deceased is included in a prayer for the redemption of the Jewish people as a whole. The pious Jewish male is buried in his *tallith* (prayer shawl). It is not appropriate to send flowers for Jewish funerals.

NOTES

Korean Americans

Korean Americans
SUMMARY

Demographics

- The number of Korean Americans in the United States rose from 798,849 in 1990 to 1.246 million in 2005.
- The most Korean-populated state is California, followed by New York. The largest Korean market is Los Angeles, followed by New York City.

Cultural Insights

- Korean society, even in the United States, retains a strong Confucian tradition, which manifests in devotion to the family and the emphasis on hierarchy in relationships. However, this tradition has been modified to adapt to modern conditions.
- Overall, Korean communication is more formal than typical Western communication.
  - Important Korean holidays include the Lunar New Year, Buddha's Birthday and *Ch'sok*.

Business Practices: Dos and Don'ts

Dos

- Take time to talk to your counterpart. Your first meeting should be solely for that purpose. Never jump right into business discussions.
- Koreans bow formally at the beginning and end of a meeting. An exit bow that is longer than the greeting bow is an indication that the meeting went well.
- The basis for a successful business relationship with a Korean American is a respectful rapport between individuals. Personal relationships take precedence over business. Be sincere and honest in business dealings. Meet face to face and keep in touch after your meeting by mail, e-mail and telephone.
- Attempts by non-Koreans to adhere to Korean modes of etiquette will not go unnoticed and might be instrumental in your eventual business success.

Don'ts

- Do not sign a contract or write a person's name in red ink. This indicates that the person is deceased.
- Modesty is highly important in Korean culture. Be modest about your position and accomplishments in your company, and if you receive a compliment, politely refute it.
- Do not confuse Korean history and culture with those of any of its Asian neighbors. Korea has a distinctive language, history and culture, and Koreans are quite proud of this.

Korean Americans

Demographics

The Korean population in the United States rose from 798,849 in 1990 to 1.246 million in 2005.

The 10 most Korean populated states in 2005 were:

1. California (401,980)
2. New York (124,614)
3. New Jersey (83,981)
4. Illinois (61,441)
5. Virginia (56,224)
6. Texas (55,111)
7. Washington (51,929)
8. Maryland (41,367)
9. Georgia (37,900)
10. Pennsylvania (37,242)

The top 10 Korean markets in the United States are:

1. Los Angeles (259,479) *
2. New York (166,981)
3. San Francisco (56,807) *
4. Washington (54,717) *
5. Chicago (46,201)
6. Seattle (42,698) *
7. Philadelphia (32,769)
8. Honolulu (23,536)
9. Atlanta (23,389)
10. Dallas (18,237)

Includes surrounding cities

Cultural Insights

Worldview

- Korean culture centers around a belief in being faithful to personal duties.

- Koreans are known for taking pride in their work ethic.

- Koreans respect their elders for their influence and accomplishments.

Sense of Self

- Koreans have a strong sense of history and a strong will. Throughout their history, Koreans have endured pain and suffering that came from foreign invasions and internal wars. Such a difficult life made the Koreans survivors. The concept of *ukjee*, a Korean word that means to force or to make happen, captures the essence of the Korean fighting spirit and will to survive.
- Koreans value interpersonal relationships. *Inyun* translates roughly as bonding, interpersonal relationship and affinity. Koreans believe that the relationship that develops between two people takes place not by accident but by destiny. Trusted relationships have had a powerful meaning for this culture because throughout history Koreans have had to rely on trusted individuals to survive in a harsh world.

Sense of Space

- Koreans typically need more space in interpersonal interactions than people from Western cultures.

Communication Style

- Overall, Korean communication is more formal than typical Western communication.

- Elderly people are highly respected, so it is good manners to greet and speak to them first and then spend a few minutes chatting with them.

- Koreans are known to be sensitive to the context of a communication. Contextual factors include the rank and age of the speaker and his/her tone of voice.

- Koreans are known to practice indirect communication. Thus, "Yes," does not always mean agreement. It might mean that the listener does not want to embarrass the speaker by not agreeing. The answer of "yes" might also be an attempt to avoid embarrassing themselves by admitting that they do not understand what has been said.

Eye Contact

- Typically, unacculturated Korean men greet each other with a slight bow and sometimes an accompanying handshake, while at the same time maintaining eye contact. The junior person will initiate the greeting and be the first to bow. The senior person will be the first to offer his hand and, at the same time, maintain eye contact. One can indicate added respect by supporting the right forearm with the left hand during the handshake.

- Eye contact is important to convey sincerity and attentiveness to the speaker.

- Do not confuse eye contact with staring. Koreans tend to make periodic eye contact during a conversation.

Language

- Koreans all speak and write the same language, which has been a crucial factor in their strong national identity. There are several different dialects, but they are similar enough so that speakers have little trouble understanding each other. The Korean language belongs to the Ural-Altaic group, which also includes Turkish, Hungarian, Finnish, Mongolian and Japanese.

- The written alphabet, *Hangeul*, was developed by a group of scholars at the behest of King Sejong the Great (whose rule lasted from 1418 to 1450), the fourth monarch of the Josun Dynasty (1392-1910). *Hangeul* consists of 10 vowels and 14 consonants, which can be combined to form numerous syllabic groupings. It is easy to learn and to write. These factors have greatly contributed to the high literacy rate among Koreans.

- The most commonly spoken forms of Korean in business are polite and honorific. The honorific form is used to acknowledge the other person's status and give them respect. The polite form is used when a person is discussing matters related to himself or herself by lowering his/her status. For non-Korean speakers, the overall use of formal rather than colloquial language and polite behavior is more appropriate.

- Census data in 2005 reported that 80 percent of Korean Americans speak Korean in the home.

Time and Time Consciousness

- Punctuality is valued in Korea. Most often, the participants arrive before the actual meeting time to show their sincerity. Even in America, Koreans believe that it is good manners to arrive early rather than making others wait for them.

Values and Norms

- For centuries, education was the only means of upward mobility in Korea. With the Chinese institution of the state examination system that screened prominent Confucian scholars for high government posts, education became the only route to political and financial success. The value of education remains ingrained in the collective unconsciousness of Koreans.

- Typically, for Korean Americans, family interests most often come before the interests of the individual.

- Children are taught from an early age that everything they do reflects on their family. Thus, Korean Americans usually try to conduct themselves in a manner that will honor their family and their ancestors.

- Korean society, even in the United States, retains a strong Confucian tradition, which is clearly manifested in the profound devotion to the family and the emphasis on hierarchy and vertical relationships. For example, the role of the unacculturated Korean male in the family typically does not include helping with domestic chores around the house and helping to raise the children.

Business Practices: Dos and Don'ts

Dos

- Take time to talk to your counterpart. Your first meeting should be solely for the purpose of getting to know one another. Never jump right into business discussions.

- Age and rank are important in Korean culture. It is sometimes easier to establish a business relationship with a person your own age.

- Negotiations with an unacculturated Korean American business person can be much more emotionally expressive than with Westerners, who usually stress logic and bottom line cost. Mutual trust and compatibility will be the basis of a good business relationship.

Also, be prepared for the style of your counterpart to possibly be aggressive at times, with emotions expressed during negotiations. Korean Americans can be direct and quick to express anger or frustration. Remain calm yourself, and do not take everything said during these sessions personally.

- The basis for a successful business relationship with an unacculturated Korean American is a respectful rapport between individuals. Personal relationships take precedence over business. People who are in businesses are basically conservative and have a strong work ethic. Harmony and structure are emphasized over innovation and experimentation. Be sincere and honest in business dealings. Meet face to face and keep in touch after your meeting by mail, e-mail and telephone.

- Attempts by non-Koreans to adhere to Korean modes of etiquette will not go unnoticed and might be instrumental in your eventual business success.

Don'ts

- Modesty is highly important in Korean culture. Be modest about your position and accomplishments in your company, and if you receive a compliment, politely refute it. Expect others to do the same. This should not stop you from complimenting another, however, because compliments are appreciated.

- Do not confuse Korean history and culture with those of any of its Asian neighbors. Korea has a distinctive language, history and culture, and Koreans are quite proud of this. This pride and sense of history are strong and constitute a large part of their self-image. Koreans are especially sensitive about Japan (because of wars, atrocities and repressive colonization), so do not bring gifts from Japan or make reference to personal contacts there.

- Do not sign a contract or write a person's name in red ink. This indicates that the person is deceased.

- Saving "face"—the dignity of another person—is an important and delicate matter. Therefore, never embarrass another person, especially in public. Never criticize your competition or admit that you do not know the answer to a question.

- Blowing your nose in public is considered bad manners.

- Since a majority of Korean Americans are Christian and many attend church and Bible study groups on Wednesday evenings, it is best to avoid Wednesdays when planning business and social functions.

Historical Background

Korea's original name, Chosun, meant "land of the morning calm". This seems paradoxical because the country's history has been shaped by frequent invasions from its neighbors. Korean history is divided into three main periods: the Shilla (668-935), Koryo (935-1392), and Yi (1392-1910) dynasties. The name, Korea, is derived from the middle dynasty of Koryo. Foreign influence, direct and indirect, occurred throughout these dynasties. All of Korea's foreign overlords (Mongolian, Chinese and Japanese) instituted a closed-door policy in order to solidify their rule. This isolation earned Korea the name of the Hermit Kingdom.

In 1910, Japan annexed Korea and enforced ruthless control, outlawing the Korean culture and language. After the Japanese lost World War II, the occupation of Korea ended. Japanese forces south of the 38th parallel, which is the degree of latitude that presently divides North and South Korea, surrendered to the United States, and forces in the north surrendered to the U.S.S.R. The Soviets blocked attempts to hold nationwide elections, and the two sides became deadlocked. When authorities in the north ignored a United Nations resolution for supervised elections in 1948, a pro-Western government was established in the south (the Republic of Korea). Later, the Soviet Union established the Democratic People's Republic of Korea in the north. In June 1949, U.S. troops withdrew.

One year later, North Korean forces invaded South Korea. The result was the Korean War and a terrible loss of life for both combatants and innocent civilians. The resulting conflict lasted three years and ended in a stalemate. On July 27, 1953, an armistice agreement was signed, and a Military Armistice Commission with five members for each side was set up to supervise the implementation of the truce. Because neither the United States nor South Korea ever signed the agreement (although they respect the terms as members of the United Nations), a state of war is formally still in effect.

The United States still maintains a military presence in South Korea, although native feelings that this should end are growing intensely. The two countries remain strong allies and trading partners.

Immigration to the United States

Koreans chose to immigrate to America for a variety of reasons. Motivations varied based on circumstances in both Korea and the United States. Those motivations can be divided into push and pull factors. Push factors are those that cause a group of people to consider leaving their homeland. Pull factors are those that entice a group of people to choose America as their destination.

The first wave of Korean immigrants (1903-1905) left their homeland and came to Hawaii in response to a labor shortage on sugar plantations because of the Chinese Exclusion Act of 1882. The promise of well-paying jobs in Hawaii away from the tyrannical rule of the Japanese acted as the pull factor for this first group of immigrants. Most of these first immigrants intended to return to Korea after making a desired amount of money working in Hawaii. The duration of this first wave was so short because Korea was officially annexed to the Japanese empire in 1910. Thus, Koreans became Japanese nationals and, as such, were excluded from entering the United States by the Gentleman's Agreement of 1908.

There have been several U.S. immigration laws affecting Asians over the years. The Immigration Act of 1924 grew out of the Quota Act of 1921, limiting the total number of immigrants to 150,000 per year, of which Japan was allowed only 185. Quotas for Asian countries were never filled because of a discriminatory clause in the law stating "no alien ineligible for citizenship shall be admitted." Eligibility, at that time, was limited to White people, people of African descent, and people of races indigenous to the Western Hemisphere.

The Immigration Law of 1924, often called the Oriental Exclusion Law, even banned spouses of Asian-American citizens. These laws effectively ended Korean immigration for decades.

The main push factors motivating the second wave (1951-1964) of immigrants to leave Korea were the chaos and strife caused by the Korean War. Pull factors for this wave included the McCarran and Walters Act of 1952, which retained the quota system but allowed Asians to immigrate to the United States and gain citizenship. This act also established a preference for highly skilled workers and relatives of U.S. citizens. Furthermore, the War Brides Act of 1946 admitted alien wives and children of U.S. servicemen on a nonquota basis. Thus, Korean War brides (6,400) and children made up the bulk of this wave of immigrants. Another large segment of this wave consisted of 5,300 war orphans adopted by American couples with the help of Harry and Bertha Holt, who pressed for laws allowing international adoption. Approximately 2,300 professional workers and students were also admitted during this period.

Push factors for the third wave of immigrants (1965 and after) included the division of the Korean peninsula into North and South, which split many Korean families. Fear and frustration over this turn of events caused many to leave Korea. As with all wars, the loss of life, destruction of property and loss of jobs would haunt Korea for years. Many Koreans fled to escape this loss and recuperate financially.

In the mid-1960s, South Korean President Park Chung Hee pushed a plan to industrialize the Korean economy and focus on exports. South Korea had little capital or technology and, therefore, had to rely heavily on the United States and Japan, which led to increased Korean dependence on international financial markets.

The military government of this era accepted financial contributions from *chaebol*, business conglomerates, and offered special favors in return, such as tax evasion and price fixing. This corruption led to a weakening of small and medium-size businesses, forcing many Koreans out of work. This, in turn, led to a mass exodus of businesspeople and white-collar workers from Korea. Many urban, middle-class Koreans who could afford to leave did so.

More recently, the economic crisis that hit Asia in the 1990s caused a new surge in immigration. Uncertain of their future, many have chosen to leave the country to look for newer and better opportunities.

Pull factors for this wave started with the Immigration Act of 1965, which abolished the quota based on nationality. The new quotas changed to 120,000 from the Western Hemisphere and 170,000 from the Eastern Hemisphere, with a maximum of 20,000 from any individual country.

Immediate relatives of American citizens were not subject to the quota. This provision carved the path for chain migration of family members. This law also established a preference for immigrants in professions needed in the United States, including physicians, nurses and engineers.

Religion

Korean American Christianity

Affiliation with the Christian church is one of the major defining characteristics of Korean Americans. Korean Americans rapidly assimilated Christianity as their dominant religion because so many of them had been exposed to and even converted to Christianity before their migration. In fact, American Christian missionaries, who often helped convert them, encouraged many of the earlier immigrants to come to the United States. Half of recent immigrants were already Christian when they were living in Korea.

Today, approximately 75 percent of Korean immigrants in the United States go to Korean immigrant churches. These Christian Korean American churches are a central factor for maintaining ethnic and cultural ties. Christian Koreans frequently attend church and Bible study groups on Wednesday evenings. It might be best, therefore, to avoid Wednesdays when planning business and social functions.

Korean American Buddhism

Approximately 8 percent of Korean Americans attend Buddhist temples in the United States. Korean Americans who are Buddhist are mainly elderly, first-generation immigrants. But even at Buddhist temples, Korean Americans have adopted many of the Christian habits of worship, such as Sunday services, organ music, hymns, sermons and Sunday school.

The Korean American Market

The Korean American segment is the most homogeneous group of the Asian Americans in the United States. Large-scale Korean immigration, including many entire families, began during the late 1960s. As a result, Korean Americans, like other ethnicities, can be segmented by generation. The first generation is *il-se* adult immigrants. Then there are *il-jom-o-se* or "one-point-five" generation. Finally, there is *i-se*, which is second generation. Although there might be many differences between parents and children, the identity of Korean Americans is strongly rooted in their native culture.

Degree of Acculturation

In general, many Korean Americans have maintained their cultural identity rather than adopting the characteristics of mainstream America. Rather than becoming highly assimilated to American culture, these individuals have blended their own cultural heritage with that of the American culture in a process called "adhesive adaptation". Thus, while a Korean could take on the outward trappings of American culture (enjoying basketball and McDonalds, for instance), he still feels and honors the importance and deep meaning of his Korean heritage.

Holidays and Celebrations

It is important to note that many Korean Americans have also adopted Thanksgiving, Christmas and New Year s Day as important holidays. Also, a lot of Korean Americans visit their families in Korea during major holidays.

New Year's Day (*Shin Jung*): The first two days of the New Year are celebrated as a time for family gatherings. Various traditional folk ceremonies and celebrations are also held.

Lunar New Year's Day (*Goo Jung*): One of the most important events of the year, it is celebrated in a similar way to Jan. 1, but on a grander scale. In Korea, most businesses are closed and people will take several days off to visit their hometowns. Many families perform ceremonies to honor their ancestors, and there is much eating of traditional foods and playing of folk games. In the United States, families gather to celebrate their ancestors with ritualistic dinners. Incense is burned. Fruits, meat, soup and seafood are always served, along with the ancestors' favorite cuisine. This follows the Confucian tradition of honoring ancestors. These dinners are traditionally held in the evening and would not affect business.

Lunar Moon Festival: The New Year celebration continues with the Lunar Moon Festival. This is observed on the 15th day of the Lunar New Year and is the day when the moon is at its fullest. Korean families and communities will often gather to celebrate and eat traditional dishes. One meal eaten on this occasion is five-grain rice, a healthy rice dish made with several types of beans and other grains.

Buddha's Birthday: Elaborate and solemn rituals are held at many Buddhist temples across the country, and lanterns are displayed in the streets and in temple courtyards. In the evening, these lanterns are carried in parades. Korean businesspeople who are Buddhist would, in all probability, not attend business functions on this date.

Ch'usok: This is the Korean Thanksgiving Day/Harvest Moon Festival and the most important traditional holiday of the year. It is celebrated on the 15th day of the eighth lunar month to herald the harvest and to give thanks for the bounty of the earth. People visit their family tombs to present offerings to their ancestors with the year's new crops and fruits.

NOTES

Mexican Americans

Mexican Americans
SUMMARY

Demographics

- The number of Mexicans in the United States increased 210 percent from 13.5 million (1990) to 41.9 million (2005).
- The largest Mexican populations are found in the West (54.2 percent) and the South (32.7 percent). The majority of Mexicans live in California.
- The five largest Mexican populations in the United States are found in Los Angeles, Houston, San Antonio, Chicago and Phoenix.

Cultural Insights

- With unacculturated Mexican Americans, the emotional impact of an interaction can be more important than the objective information and facts. This is particularly important in the context of sales, where developing a relationship based on an emotional connection can make the difference between success and failure.
- As compared to typical Western communication style, communication among Mexicans is more indirect. Indirect communication is used to avoid offending others.
- Propriety is highly important, especially the perception of what other people might misconstrue as rude behavior. In traditional Mexican culture, it is important to "save face", while at the same time not embarrassing anybody else.
- Mexican men greet each other with a handshake and, sometimes, after they have established a relationship, an accompanying hug. For women, a pat on the forearm or shoulder is the norm. Kissing on the cheek is also an acceptable salutation in public once relationships have been established. Remember, however, that the culture is conservative, so it is important to avoid any behavior that might appear sexual in nature.
- The major holidays practiced by Mexicans in the United States are: *Cinco de Mayo* (May 5), Independence Day (Sept. 16), *Dia De los Muertos* (Day of the Dead, Nov. 1) and the Christmas holidays.

Business Practices: Dos and Don'ts

Dos

- For unacculturated Mexicans in general, time is not as finite as it typically is in U.S. culture. Punctuality, although admired, is not strictly adhered to in daily life.
- *Personalismo* (personalism): When engaging in business, Mexicans often look for long-term relationships based on mutual trust and reliability. They are known to expect personal attention, which can be perceived as more important than the product or the prestige of the company.
- Admit when you have made a mistake. This can be valuable in developing a necessary relationship.

- *Acomodandose a mis necesidades* (accommodating my needs): When dealing with unacculturated Mexican consumers, one must often be as flexible and accommodating as possible. The unacculturated place a premium on flexibility. They are accustomed to systems that bend the rules to accommodate their needs.

Don'ts

- Indirectness in communication is valuable as a way to maintain social harmony. A flat-out "no", therefore, can have negative connotations. Instead, words like "maybe" or "we will see" might take its place in order to be polite.
- Privacy is an important value and individual dignity is valued, regardless of social standing or wealth. Avoid publicly embarrassing or criticizing anyone, as this might make the individual withdraw.
- If you are invited to the home of an unacculturated Mexican family, do not expect to discuss business unless otherwise prompted. Utilize this time to get to know the family.

Mexican Americans

Demographics

The number of Mexicans in the United States increased 210 percent from 13.5 million (1990) to 41.9 million (2005). The largest Mexican populations are found in the West (54.2 percent) and the South (32.7 percent).

The 10 most Mexican populated States in 2005 were:

1. California (10,352,618)
2. Texas (6,583,095)
3. Arizona (1,481,707)
4. Illinois (1,418,049)
5. Colorado (652,387)
6. Florida (531,902)
7. Nevada (449,767)
8. Washington (444,174)
9. New Mexico (442,799)
10. Georgia (417,452)

The largest Mexican populations in 2005 in the United States were found in the following cities:

1. Los Angeles (1,254,396)
2. Houston (624,652)
3. San Antonio (594,082)
4. Chicago (564,853)
5. Phoenix (524,395)

Cultural Insights

Worldview

- Unacculturated Mexican Americans tend to be firmly oriented in the here and now, and value enjoying life in the present. As for the future, obedience to the will of God, instilled through Catholic upbringing, will secure good tidings.

- The emotional impact of an interaction can be more important than the objective information and facts. This is particularly important in the context of sales, where developing a relationship based on an emotional connection can make the difference between success and failure.

- Many Latinos' thought processes—in contrast to American thinking, which places strong emphasis on self-control in shaping the future—are manifested by an external locus of control. That is, Mexicans often believe that their future is in the hands of an outside force, such as God, and that they are powerless to alter their fate. A famous saying is *lo que sera, sera* ("whatever will be, will be"). Another well-known expression that conveys this message is *si Dios quiere* ("If God wills it").

Sense of Self

- Traditionally, Mexicans have demonstrated a strong preference for the status quo. Mexican culture has an aversion to any radical changes. Political scientists use this as one explanation for the longevity of the PRI as the sole political party in control of the Mexican presidency for most of the 20th century. This preference for the status quo should not be confused with laziness, as there is strong emphasis on hard work in this culture.

- Mexicans frequently place value on the past, particularly the history of the family. The family unit is the most important societal factor and plays a crucial role in the perception of self. The individual is responsible for his/her decisions, but the best interest of the family or group is a dominating factor. It is important for one to know a person before conducting business with him or her. A good way to know a Mexican is to know his/her family.

- Value is placed on interpersonal relationships. Traditionally, the ability to foster and maintain good personal relationships has been viewed as essential.

- Gender roles are clearly defined. Although Mexican Americans have been influenced by contemporary social, liberal philosophies such as feminism, with the unnaculterated, *machismo* is still pervasive.

Sense of Space

- Mexicans, in general, are comfortable with close contact. Affection is demonstrated freely. Conversations might take place at a closer distance than what would be considered comfortable in the United States. Maintaining distance can be taken as an indication of avoidance or rejection.

- Initial formality, as with other cultures, is emphasized as a sign of respect. Once those boundaries are set and friendships develop, propriety might give way to more friendly and informal interaction.

Communication Style

- As compared to Western communication, expression is more indirect, so as not to offend. Propriety is important—specially the perception of what other people might misconstrue as rude behavior. It is important to "save face", while at the same time not embarrassing anybody else.

- Emphasis is placed on careful listening. This type of attention demonstrates that one is focusing on what the speaker is saying. The culture values the attention a listener gives to the individual who is speaking.

- Spontaneous expression of emotion is deemed as appropriate and acceptable in particular contexts.

- After they have established a relationship, Mexican men frequently greet each other with a handshake and, sometimes, an accompanying hug. For women, a pat on the forearm or shoulder is the norm. Once relationships have been established, kissing on the cheek is also an acceptable salutation in public. Remember, however, that the culture is conservative, so it is important to avoid any behavior that might appear sexual in nature.

- Elderly people are highly respected so it is good manners to initially spend a few minutes with them. Remember to greet and speak to them first.

- Loud verbal communication is avoided as it might be interpreted as an expression of anger and might cause embarrassment.

- It is seen as disrespectful and rude to disagree with someone unless you know him or her well. Contradicting someone requires the structure of an existing relationship.

- The Spanish language provides forms of formal and nonformal address (different use of *usted* vs. *tu* for the pronoun you, polite and familiar commands, and the use of titles of respect before people's first names such as *Don* or *Doña*). In nonformal settings, conversations between Spanish speakers are usually loud and fast when compared to similar English-language conversations in the United States.

Eye Contact

- Eye contact is important to convey sincerity and attentiveness to the speaker. However, among Mexicans from more traditional and rural communities, eye contact might be seen as defiant. Therefore, it is avoided in uncomfortable situations. For example, when elders are disciplining a young person, the youth is expected to bow his/her head down and not make direct eye contact. Similarly, unacculturated Mexicans will avoid direct eye contact in uncomfortable situations.

Language

- Mexicans have a common spoken and written language: Spanish. There are several different indigenous dialects spoken by some immigrants throughout the country, but those dialects are rarely utilized. Eighty-six percent of U.S. Latinos say Spanish is their first language.

- The most commonly spoken form of Spanish in business is very formal. Titles are important in Mexico. When addressing a doctor or professor, use the title. First names are only used by those who are on familiar terms. Wait for your counterpart to initiate this switch from professional to familiar terms. This same principle applies with elders and more respected counterparts.

- For the unacculturated and recent immigrants to the United States, Spanish communications are essential. With the proliferation of Spanish-language media and publications in the United States, the need to quickly assimilate English-language capability is not as urgent as it might have been for earlier generations of immigrants.

Time and Time Consciousness

- Mexicans and unacculturated Latinos in general are flexible with time. In Latino culture, time is not perceived to be finite, as is the case in U.S. culture. Rather, the focus is primarily given to the quality of the interpersonal experience. Punctuality, although admired, is not strictly adhered to in daily life.

Values and Norms

- Mexican-American cultural values and attitudes are shaped in large part by Catholic ideology. Mexican Americans attempt to hold on to their traditional Mexican values, but length of time spent in the United States and varying degrees of assimilation might affect retention of traditional values.

- *Familismo* has to do with the high degree of interpersonal bonding within the Mexican family, resulting in greater identification with the group and dependence on the family. Recent studies also have demonstrated the importance of the nuclear and extended family as a source of social support. Latinos might "adopt" close friends as *compadres* and family members in the absence of blood ties.

- *Machismo* characterizes the male gender role in Latino society. It stresses virility, independence and physical strength. It supports the idea that women are subordinate and inferior to men. However, with more exposure to North American attitudes, this belief is being questioned.

- *Marianismo* has been characterized as the complement of *machismo*. *Marianismo* defines the role of the ideal woman, modeled after the Virgin Mary, as based on chastity, renunciation and sacredness, while reinforcing obedience.

- Family. Mexican families—which tend to be larger and younger and to consist of multiple generations, in comparison with Caucasian families—are child-centric, placing a significant value on the well-being of children.

- Value of Education. Until the 1930s, public education was not available in Mexico on a nationwide scale. Considerable portions of those who have immigrated to the United States in the past three decades (1970s, 1980s and 1990s) acquired limited education in their homeland. For most of this century, only a sixth-grade education was mandatory in Mexico, with many children not even accomplishing that because of financial hardship and the necessity to start earning wages at an early age. The main reason for immigration for most Mexicans is the search for better work and educational opportunities for their children.

- Work Ethic. Most Mexican immigrants left their country in search of better work to provide for their own basic necessities and those of their families back home. With limited education and technical skills, the majority of Mexican immigrants do labor-intensive, low-paying work. The remittances sent back to Mexico total several billion dollars a year and are one of the largest sources of revenue for the whole country. Mexicans are extremely committed to working hard in order to reach success.

148

Sociologists and historians attribute this aspiration and work ethic in part to the rejection of the *mestizos* (those of mixed European and indigenous blood) who make up the majority of the Mexican population.

Business Practices: Dos and Don'ts

Dos

- For Latinos in general, time is not finite as is the case in U.S. culture. Punctuality, although admired, is not strictly adhered to in daily life. Be accommodating with your schedule, both with business and social events. Be calm and patient with delays. Plan for and expect them.

- *Personalismo* (personalism): When engaging in business, unacculturated Mexicans often seek long-term relationships based on mutual trust and reliability. The unacculturated are known to expect personal attention. For them, this attention can be more important than the product or the prestige of the company. As part of *personalismo*, high value is placed on proper social form, civility and respect. Strong business relationships are important because many unacculturated Mexicans tend to be more conservative than others. Thus, many are not likely to be "early adopters", choosing to wait for proven results before deciding on a certain product. This means that the sales cycle might be longer and that the prospect needs the comfort afforded by an established relationship in order for the necessary trial to occur. A sales rep should review the progress of his client and encourage him or her at each step. It is important to "temperature check" after each sales presentation. This usually entails being sensitive to clients' reactions to each topic, providing an in depth explanation, modifying the presentation where necessary and clearly demonstrating the product's applicability in real situations.

- *Acomodandose a mis necesidades* (accommodating my needs): When dealing with unacculturated Mexican consumers, one might need to be as flexible and accommodating as possible. The unacculturated place a premium on flexibility. They are accustomed to systems that bend the rules to accommodate their needs.

Don'ts

- Indirectness in communication is valuable as a way to maintain social harmony. A flat-out "no", therefore, has negative connotations. Thus, unacculturated Mexicans might avoid using the word. Instead, substitute words like "maybe" or "we will see", which are perceived as polite alternatives. In order to have concrete confirmation, get it in writing.

- "Saving face" and privacy are important values and individual dignity is valued, regardless of social standing or wealth. Avoid publicly embarrassing or criticizing anyone, as this might make the individual withdraw. On the other hand, admitting when you have made a mistake can be valuable in developing trust in the relationship.

- If you are invited to the home of an unacculturated Mexican family, do not expect to discuss business unless otherwise prompted. Utilize this time to get to know the family.

Historical Background

In the early 16th century, at the time of the Spanish conquest led by Hernàn Cortez, the Aztecs were the native people who dominated central Mexico. Besides the Aztecs, the population was made up of diverse groups of indigenous tribes, some of them highly sophisticated, like the Mayans in the Yucatan Peninsula and the Olmecs in central México. The variety of indigenous subcultures is still present. It resulted in a diversity of dialects, foods, architecture and cultures.

The conquest of Mexico by the Spanish decimated many of its indigenous populations, primarily through diseases such as smallpox and the common flu. What emerged from the meeting of these two worlds was what is called *mestizaje*. *Mestizaje* is the hybrid of Spanish and indigenous peoples. It created a unique set of cultural and societal norms that have affected the course of history for Mexico, as well as for most of Latin America.

What also emerged from the conquest was a concrete and rigid structure that defined the manner of conduct between different social classes. At the top of this hierarchy were the *Peninsulares*, those people born in the actual Iberian Peninsula of Spain. Right below this group were the *Criollos*, or Creoles, that is, people of Spanish blood who were born in the Americas. Beneath the *Criollos* were the *Mestizos* (the largest group of what is known today as Mexicans), the working-class masses produced by the intermarriage of European and indigenous blood. At the bottom of this order were the marginalized indigenous populations who were relegated to engaging in most menial and backbreaking labor. This social order continued to exist throughout Mexican history. Just as slavery and segregation in the United States played a major role in the construct of America's current perception of race, so has Mexico's utilization of this social structure shaped Mexicans' perceptions of and interactions between social classes.

After approximately three centuries of Spanish rule, Mexico began its war for independence on Sept. 16, 1810. This day is commemorated as *El Grito* ("the yell"). It is the most celebrated national holiday, much like the Fourth of July in the United States. Mexico officially became a republic in 1824.

For most of Mexico's developing history, a small minority was in control of most of the country's power and wealth, while the majority of the population worked in poverty. Long-time President Porfírio Diaz was pressured into holding an election in 1910, in which Madero, an opposition party candidate, was able to gather a significant number of the votes. Diaz had Madero imprisoned. His imprisonment led to massive discontent, and Diaz was unable to control the spread of the resulting insurgence and resigned in May 1911. He signed the Treaty of Ciudad Juarez, after which he fled to France.

Madero was elected president but encountered opposition from different political elements. It was during this time that the country broke into many different factions. Guerilla units roamed across the country destroying and burning down many large haciendas. Revolutionaries such as Emiliano Zapata and Pancho Villa gained prominence.

Eventually, Venustiano Carranza rose to the presidency and organized an important convention whose outcome was the Constitution of 1917. This document, which is modeled closely after the U.S. Constitution, is still in effect today. Carranza was followed by other leaders who would fight for political control and who would eventually continue with reforms, mostly in the educational

150

system and in land distribution. During this period, the PRI political party was established and continued to be the dominant political power in Mexico until 2000. In that year, the Partido Accion Nacional (PAN), headed by President Vicente Fox, defeated the PRI. The PRI had held the presidency for more than 70 years, making it the longest-ruling party in modern world history. Economically, a broad range of business climates exists throughout the country, from the industrial north to the more traditional and rural southeast. Mexico is also characterized by extreme economic stratification.

Immigration to the United States

At the turn of the 20th century, the rapid growth of the U.S. economy attracted Mexican immigrants as laborers. This trend continued throughout World War I. The devastation of the Mexican Revolution around this time also led to a massive displacement of refugees to the U.S. side of the border. As the Great Depression dawned and nativism arose, hundreds of thousands of Mexican Americans, many of whom were U.S. citizens, were rounded up and deported.

Another large immigration occurred during World War II, when there was a shortage of labor in the United States. The *bracero* program was created to import agricultural and other low-skilled workers from Mexico for a short period of time without offering citizenship. Although this was a temporary fix for wartime needs, the agricultural industry became dependent upon Mexican labor. The *bracero* program continued until 1964. This program brought up to 400,000 laborers into all areas of the United States annually.

Since World War II, urbanization has been the key to the forming of Mexican communities. In 1940, Mexicans were the most rural of the major ethnic groups in the United States, due primarily to migrant labor. By 1970, they were among the most urbanized.

Throughout much of the 1980s and 1990s, Mexico experienced severe economic recessions, thus prompting substantial waves of immigration, primarily to the Southwest.

Religion

The majority of Mexican Americans are Catholic, and the Catholic Church carries a great deal of significance in the overall lives of these people. This has an impact on the many rituals practiced by Mexican American families. The brand of Catholicism the Spanish introduced in Mexico cannibalized many indigenous symbols and practices in order to assure its own survival. Catholicism in Mexico has some unique elements. Most notable are the veneration of the Virgin of Guadalupe, the special importance of saints and some elements from pre-Columbian indigenous tradition.

In border areas like Southern California, evangelical religious groups such as Jehovah's Witnesses and Pentecostals have attracted a considerable number of followers among Mexican American Catholics.

The Mexican American/Latino Market

Because Mexicans make up the majority of the Latino population in the United States, they shape and mirror the national research findings on the Hispanic market. For example:

- According to the Selig Center for Economic Growth at the University of Georgia, in 1997 Latino purchasing power exceeded $860 billion.

- In 2005, only 48 percent of Latinos owned homes, compared with 74 percent of non-Hispanic Whites.

- A.C. Nielsen Corporation data show that acculturation, the process by which newcomers adapt to a different culture, has an impact on Latino buying habits. Shopping patterns in Latino households where English is the preferred or dominant language, closely parallel the general market. In homes where Spanish is the preferred or only language spoken, buying habits are noticeably different.

Degree of Acculturation

First-generation immigrants are the most tied to Mexican traditions and institutions. They are dealing with the barriers of another culture and language. Most of this generation still speaks Spanish in the home. Subsequent generations are more likely to maintain the language and cultural traditions if they are in ethnically homogeneous neighborhoods. The degree of acculturation can create problems within the family. Older family members hold the language and values of the Mexican culture dear, while the younger members become more quickly assimilated.

Although utilization of Spanish decreases through the generations, second generation (and beyond) Mexican Americans sometimes use Spanish for its emotional impact in communication. That is, they utilize English in everyday interactions, but Spanish becomes a resource for the expression of feelings that are sometimes difficult to manifest or articulate through the English language.

New immigrants to the United States are most likely to be marginalized. Additional barriers—such as understanding of language, difficulty in navigating community systems and lack of knowledge of their individual rights and fear of the authorities—can further alienate Mexican immigrants.

Economic Status

Latino immigrants generally hold manual-labor, service and support jobs. The National Research Council reports that the overall positive effect immigrants have on the economy is between $1 billion and to $10 billion dollars per year. According to the Census 2005 American Community Survey, 67 percent of Latinos have no college education, which could land them higher-paying jobs.

Holidays and Celebrations

New Year's Day (*Año Nuevo*)—Jan. 1: Traditional Western holiday.

Day of the Magi (*Día de los Santos Reyes/Magos*)—Jan. 6: Traditionally, this is this day when gifts are dispensed (as opposed to Christmas Day) to commemorate the day when the Magi presented gifts to Jesus of Nazareth. Children are instructed to leave their shoes outdoors overnight for the Magi to stuff them with gifts. The traditional *Rosca de Reyes*, a sweet oval-shaped pastry, is served at the house of the person housing the baby Jesus statuette during Christmas celebrations. The person who receives the piece of pastry with a small baby Jesus in it is supposed to host a breakfast made up of tamales and hot chocolate, or *atole*, on Candlemass Day the following month.

Easter and *La Semana Santa* (Holy Week): Easter is one of the highest holy days of the year for Latino Catholics. It is celebrated nearly everywhere in Latin America and Spain with religious observances and various types of processions. *Semana Santa* begins with Palm Sunday (*el Domingo de Ramos*), includes Good Friday (*el Viernes Santo*) and ends with Easter (*la Pascua de Resurrección*). The week is meant to mark the triumphant entry of Jesus into Jerusalem followed by his death and resurrection. One Mexican custom is to break *cascarones*, or eggshells filled with confetti, placed on someone's head as a surprise.

Battle of Puebla/ Cinco de Mayo (*La Batalla de Puebla*) May 5: Commemorates the victory over French invaders in Puebla. For the most part, the holiday of *Cinco de Mayo* is more of a regional holiday in Mexico, celebrated most vigorously in the state of Puebla. Celebrating Cinco de Mayo has become increasingly popular in parts of the United States that have a large population of people of Mexican heritage. Today's holiday has come to be a celebration of culture, food, music, beverages and customs unique to Mexico.

Mother's Day (*Día de las Madres*)—May 10: Unlike in the United States, Mother's Day is always celebrated on the 10th of May.

Independence Day (*Día de la Independencia/ El Grito*)—Sept. 16: This is the most important federal holiday. Pageantry and fireworks light up major metropolitan centers, especially Mexico City. The holiday commemorates the declaration of war against Spain in 1810 with ringing of bells.

Day of the Dead (*Día de los Muertos*)—Nov. 1: Celebrated in Mexico and in certain parts of the United States and Central America. In rural Mexico, people visit the cemeteries where their loved ones are buried. They decorate gravesites with flowers and candles. They sit on picnic blankets next to gravesites and eat the favorite food of their loved ones. This celebration originated during pre-Hispanic times. Although the ritual has since been merged with Catholic theology, it still maintains the basic principles of the Aztec ritual, such as the presentation of candy skulls.

Our Lady of Guadalupe Day (*Día de Nuestra Señora de Guadalupe*)—Dec. 12: This day commemorates the appearance of the Virgin of Guadalupe to the Indian Juan Diego on Mount Tepeyac in Mexico City in 1531. According to the accounts, Guadalupe appeared to Juan Diego, not as a European (white-skinned) Madonna, but as an indigenous (dark-skinned) reincarnation of the Virgin Mary. When Juan Diego related these accounts to the local priests, he was ridiculed and was asked to demonstrate some proof. After further meetings with Guadalupe in Tepeyac, Juan Diego was ordered by Guadalupe to gather some roses in the mantle he was wearing and to take them back to the priests. When Juan Diego released his mantle to show the roses, a life-size replica of Guadalupe was imprinted on his robe. Guadalupe was canonized by the Catholic Church and became essential in the mass conversion of the majority of the indigenous populations of Mexico. Mexico's most important cathedral now stands where the apparitions in

Tepeyac took place. It houses the imprinted robe Juan Diego wore. The symbol of Guadalupe is a recognizable religious and popular art figure both in Mexico and in the United States. Guadalupe has become the symbol of Mexican Catholicism both in Mexico and abroad. Recently, Juan Diego was canonized, as well.

Las Posadas—Dec. 16: Celebrates Joseph and Mary's search for shelter in Bethlehem with candlelight processions that end at various nativity scenes. *Las Posadas* continues through Dec. 24.

Nochebuena (Christmas Eve) and *Navidad* (Christmas)—Dec. 24-25: With the rest of the Christian world, Mexico celebrates Christmas Day. Christmas Eve (Dec. 24) is widely observed. Dinners and festivities take place on this evening rather than on Dec. 25, the traditional celebration day in the United States.

Day of Your Saint: In Mexico, the day of your saint is celebrated similarly to your birthday. Because Mexico is a Catholic country, many Mexicans' names are derived from Catholic saints (i.e., Saint Francis Day is Oct. 4, so Francisco and Francisca would celebrate their saint day at that time).

Quinceañeras: A *quinceaeñera*, or 15th-birthday celebration, is a rite of passage for young, Catholic Hispanic girls and is growing in popularity in the United States. The roots of the ceremony are found in a combination of indigenous and Spanish customs. It is meant to represent a girl's emergence into womanhood. Girls are required to attend a year of religion classes before the celebration, which usually begins with a Mass followed by a party. The celebration itself tends be extravagant and can rival a wedding in nature. The girl will wear an elaborate dress that symbolizes femininity; a gold medallion that expresses her faith; a ring that represents her spiritual and communal responsibilities; and a crown that symbolizes her living a Christian life. She will have 14 maids of honor, or *damas* (one for each year of childhood), and each will have a male escort—all of whom will perform a symbolic dance for the occasion. These events can cost thousands of dollars, and friends and relatives will often help with the expenses.

NOTES

Muslim Americans

Muslim Americans
SUMMARY

Demographics

•   The number of Muslims in the United States is estimated to be between 5 million and 8 million.

Cultural Insights

•   Every adult Muslim is required to pray five times a day.
•   The holy day is Friday. Muslims might take a couple of hours to go to the mosque on that day.
•   It is not allowed in Islam to take persons of the opposite gender as very close friends.
•   For some, any touching between nonfamily members of the opposite sex is socially unacceptable. For others, contact is OK (i.e., a handshake) as long as it has no sexual overtones.
•   Dietary restrictions can vary between cultures. In general, Muslim diets avoid products containing pork, pork byproducts or alcohol. Most Muslims will not eat shellfish, and some believe meat must be *halal*, or from animals slaughtered in a prescribed manner. Some follow a Kosher or vegetarian diet.
•   The traditional Muslim greeting is *Al-salaamu 'alaykum* ("May peace be on you") and is responded with *wa 'alayka al-salaam* ("and on you be peace").
•   Direct eye contact is important among people of the same sex. Direct eye contact between members of the opposite sex is usually avoided among traditional Muslims.
•   The major Muslim holidays are *Ramadan*, *Eid Al-Fitr* and *Eid Al-Adha*.

Business Practices: Dos and Don'ts

Dos

•   Understand that Muslim cultures are varied around the world (i.e., Persian, Pakistani, Indonesian, Arab). One should be careful not to lump all Islamic groups into one category. Furthermore, not all Arab Americans are Muslim. (In fact, most Arab Americans are Catholic or Orthodox Christian.)
•   Be punctual for all meetings.
•   Try to arrange appointments well in advance. A personal introduction (or at least a letter of introduction) is of great assistance.
•   Respect elders. When entering a room, acknowledge the oldest person first.
•   Politeness is important. Meetings might start slowly, with small talk.
•   Eat, drink and shake hands with your right hand. In traditional Muslim cultures, the belief is prevalent that the right side is the good side (Hence, Arabic is written from right to left, and shaking one's right hand is a sign of good faith and respect).

Don'ts

- Avoid stereotyping. The Muslim world is divided by class and social structures, political systems, cultures, ethnic and racial identities, and differing histories. Avoid usage of racial categories that are common in the United States.
- If possible, avoid scheduling appointments on Fridays, especially in the early afternoon. Mid-day Friday prayers are significant for observant Muslims.
- Never make jokes about politics or sex.
- Don't give gifts made with pork products or byproducts. To be safe, avoid any meat products. Avoid gifts containing alcohol or alcohol derivatives, as well.

Muslim Americans

Demographics

At present, the number of Muslims in the United States is estimated to be between 5 million and 8 million. Many claim that Islam is the fastest-growing religion in the country. Estimates indicate that the number of Muslims in the United States will double by the year 2010.

The 10 most Muslim populated states are:

1. California
2. New York
3. Illinois
4. New Jersey
5. Indiana
6. Michigan
7. Virginia
8. Texas
9. Ohio
10. Maryland

Cultural Insights

Worldview

• The religion of Islam is the primary source of values and direction for its adherents.

• The practice of Islam is an all-encompassing way of life and can be more than a religion to its followers. It is entwined in every facet of a Muslim's life, including birth, marriage, family, death, political worldview, economics and social relationships.

• Muslims believe that people are created equal under the law of God and that it is important to have mutual respect for another human being.

Sense of Self

• The individual is typically subordinate to the family or group.

• For the religiously devout, the answers to all problems lie in the correct interpretation of divine law.

Sense of Space

• An expression frequently used in the Middle East is "I want you so close to me I can feel your breath on my cheek." This reflects the behavior of some Muslim men from the Middle East who will speak at a closer distance than might be comfortable in U.S. culture. However, Muslims come from many countries around the world. Their behavior will reflect the sense of space appropriate to the areas from which they emigrated.

Communication Style

- For some more conservative Muslims, any touching between nonfamily members of the opposite sex is socially unacceptable. For others, contact is OK (i.e., a handshake) as long as it has no sexual overtones.

- Attempt to avoid seclusion with a person from the opposite sex as it might cause the perception of temptation, which would provide an opportunity for inappropriate intimacy.

- The traditional Muslim greeting is *Al-salaamu 'alaykum* ("May peace be on you") and is responded to with *wa 'alayka al-salaam* ("and on you be peace"). While for some Muslims it is permissible to initiate the greeting to a non-Muslim, a Muslim will most likely respond to the greeting from a non-Muslim with "and on you be peace." Be careful, however, to pronounce *al-salaamu 'alaykum* correctly, because *as-saam 'alaykum* means "May death be upon you", and might be responded to with *wa'alaykum* or *'alayk* ("and upon you.").

Eye Contact

- Direct eye contact is important among people of the same sex.

- Direct eye contact between members of the opposite sex is usually avoided. This is especially true between unrelated men and women.

Language

- The use of their native languages in the home is high among the foreign-born but wanes with later generations. For example, nearly half of all Arab Americans who are 18 years and older speak a language other than English at home. The high percentage of Arabs speaking Arabic at home is likely due to more recent waves of immigration. Less than 10 percent of the population, however, does not speak English well. Bilingualism is common, and English is spoken in business practices dealing with outside communities. While the languages of Muslim immigrants might differ (for example, Iranians speak Farsi, the Persian language), this general trend is true among other Muslim immigrants, as well.

- While many Middle Eastern and South Asian Muslims use in-language media (television, radio, newspapers and magazines in their native languages), it is highly likely that those in the professional ranks will be fluent in English.

Time and Time Consciousness

- *In sha'allah* : This phrase means that when a person plans for the future and makes promises, resolutions and pledges, he makes them with permission and the will of Allah. For this reason, Muslims often say "*In sha'allah.*" The meaning of this statement is, "If Allah wills." Muslims are to strive hard and to put their trust in Allah. They leave the results in the hands of God. This phrase implies that Muslims view time not as a finite commodity, but that things occur when and if Allah wills them to occur. Thus, the pace of business might be delayed or immediate.

- Punctuality is not traditionally considered a virtue. Your business associate might be late for an appointment. You, however, should always be prompt, as more westernized Muslims will be punctual.

Values and Norms

- Many traditional Muslim groups often find it difficult to accept any outside information that does not reflect Islamic values. As with the other observant groups, problems are approached subjectively according to Islamic law.

- Muslim immigrants place a high value on education and economic mobility.

- Islam has strict regulations guiding economic life. According to Muslim faith, wealth, earnings and material goods are the property of Allah. The principles of Islam aim at establishing a just society wherein everyone will behave responsibly and honestly. Some of the fundamental principles of the Islamic economic system are as follows:

  Muslims are not to collect, charge or pay interest for loans or investments.
  A Muslim should be responsible when spending money. Extravagance and waste are strongly discouraged.
  Muslims are encouraged to give constantly to charity.
  Once a year, Muslims give Zakat (tithe), which is 2.5 percent of net savings for the previous year. This is to be given to the poor and needy.

Religious/Cultural Practices and Beliefs

- As with other religious groups, you will find individuals whose practice of Islam manifests various degrees of observance. This will entail everything from the devout to the nonobservant. For example, Saudis are especially known for their religious conservatism. They generally belong to the Wahabi sect, which is extremely conservative in its practice of Islam.

- Every adult Muslim is required to do *Sala* (prescribed prayers) five times a day. Before sunrise but after dawn is the time for the morning or *Fajr* prayer. Immediately after the meridian is the beginning of early afternoon or *Zuhr* prayer which lasts midway to sunset. From midway to sunset until shortly before sunset is the midafternoon or *'Asr* prayer time. Immediately after sunset is the *Maghrib* prayer time, which lasts until the disappearance of twilight (approximately an hour). After *Maghrib* and until dawn is the *'Isha* or night prayer time. Each of the prayers lasts five to 10 minutes and must be done within its own time slot. A brief washing is required as a preparation for the prayers.

- Although they have designated assembly places for worship (mosques), Muslims are free to pray anywhere because the entire world is considered a place of worship.

- The holy day for Muslims is Friday. In the United States, observant Muslims often take a couple of hours from their jobs or businesses to go to the mosque on Friday. The Friday prayer, held in the early afternoon, generally lasts for less than an hour.

- The Koran indicates that all Muslims should dress conservatively. Some Muslim women choose to cover their hair, although this is a cultural tradition and is not specifically addressed in the Koran. Muslim women who wear the style of dress covering the entire body, do not consider it oppressive, but many consider it liberating. In this way, they are judged on their character as opposed to their appearance. The word *hijab* can refer to head or body covering. However, a *burqua* is the term reserved for a garment that covers the entire body.

- Dietary restrictions can vary between cultures. In general, Muslim diets avoid products containing pork, pork byproducts or alcohol. Most Muslims will not eat shellfish, and some believe meat must be *halal*, or from animals slaughtered in a prescribed manner. Some follow a Kosher or vegetarian diet.

- Many Muslims do not consider the Nation of Islam (an exclusively African American group) as being Islamic.

Business Practices: Dos and Don'ts

Dos

- Understand that Muslim cultures are varied around the world (i.e., Persian, Pakistani, Indonesian, Arab). One should be careful not to lump all Islamic groups into one category. Furthermore, not all Arab Americans are Muslim. (In fact, most Arab Americans are Catholic or Orthodox Christian.)

- Be punctual for all meetings.

    Try to arrange appointments well in advance. A personal introduction (or at least a letter of introduction) is of great assistance.

- Respect elders. When entering a room, acknowledge the oldest person first.

- Politeness is important. Meetings might start slowly and with a lot of small talk. Follow the lead of your counterpart and, if possible, do not cut it short.

- Eat, drink and shake hands with your right hand. In traditional Muslim cultures, the belief is prevalent that the right side is the good or better side. (Hence, Arabic is written from right to left, and shaking one's right hand is a sign of good faith and respect.)

Don'ts

- Avoid stereotyping. The Muslim world is divided by class and social structures, political systems, cultures, ethnic and racial identities, and differing histories. Muslims are usually barraged with negative images in the U.S. media, where talk of Islam and terrorism often go hand in hand.

- Avoid scheduling appointments during major Muslim holidays.

- If possible, avoid scheduling appointments on Fridays, especially in the early afternoon. (Friday prayers offered at midday are highly significant to the observant Muslim and are equivalent in importance to the Judeo-Christian Sabbath).

- Never make jokes about politics or sex.

- When speaking to a male, do not bring up the subject of women and do not inquire as to the health of female family members.

- It is forbidden for observant Muslims to take persons of the opposite gender as close friends.

- Don't give gifts made with pork or pork by-products. To be safe, avoid any meat products as they might not be prepared in the appropriate way. Many cheeses, cookies and other foods can be unacceptable (*haram*) if they are made with animal fats. Be aware that a range of products besides food items could be considered unclean to traditional Muslims. These can include many cosmetics and skin-care items that are made with pork by-products.

- If you're joining your Muslim associate for a meal, be aware that pork is forbidden. Some are quite strict about eating only *halal* (killed and prepared in a certain way) meat. Others might be comfortable with eating non-*halaal* meat, provided it does not contain any pork. It is important to ask before making any assumptions.

- Avoid alcoholic gifts.

History of Islam

A Muslim is a practitioner of the Islamic religion. According to the Koran, Islam means "to surrender to the will or law of God". The Islamic religion was founded in Arabia and is based on the teachings of the Prophet Muhammad. At the age of 40, Muhammad claimed that the archangel Gabriel came to him in a vision. He began his ministry in Mecca and was eventually recognized as a lawgiver and prophet. Muhammad's teachings were based on generosity, justice, and the goodness, omnipotence and unity of God. While important elements from Judaism and Christianity were incorporated into the emergent religion, it was rooted in the pre-Islamic, Arabic tradition.

One of the fundamental sources of Islamic doctrine is the Koran (*Arabic Qu'ran*). The Koran is the speech of God to Muhammad, mediated through Gabriel during the 22 years of his prophetic life. It is divided into 114 chapters (*suras*) and contains the Islamic religious, social, civil, commercial, military and legal codes. There is only one version of the Koran, and the original is in Arabic. The Koran is regarded as above criticism, and copies of it are treated with great reverence. (They are never held below the girth and are not touched without prior purification of the person.)

As described in the Koran, there are five pillars in the Islamic faith that act as guidelines for Muslim living:

- Faith in one God (*Allah*) and his messenger (*Shahada*).
- Prayer five times per day while facing Mecca, the holy city in Saudi Arabia (*Salat*).
- Purifying or alms tax (i.e., mandatory giving to the poor) (*Zakat*).
- Ramadan: This is the fast conducted from dawn to sunset during the ninth month of the lunar year (*Saum*).
- Pilgrimage to Mecca at least once in a lifetime (*Hajj*).

A secondary source of Islam is the *Sunna*, or example of the Prophet. It is known through the *Hadith*, which is a body of traditions based on what Muhammad said or did. Since *Hadith* was mainly transmitted through an oral tradition, the Sunna is not considered to be infallible.

The *Sharia*, or Islamic law, explains the moral goals of the community. Islamic law is based on four sources. The first two are the Koran and Sunna. The third source, *ijtihad*, refers to "responsible individual opinion" and is used when an issue is not covered in the Koran or Sunna. Traditionally, it has been employed in integrating local customs and laws with the Koran and Sunna. The fourth source is *ijma*, the consensus of the community. Consensus is usually reached by gradually discarding some opinions and accepting others, which can take a long period of time.

Sunni Muslims, or Sunnites, make up the majority of the world's Islamic community. Sunni theology tends to maintain a more inclusive definition of a Muslim and accommodates minor differences of opinion to affirm Islam community consensus. The Shiites are the second largest Muslim sect and emerged out of dispute over the succession of Muhammad. In contrast to orthodox Sunnites, they tend to emphasize esoteric knowledge rather than community consensus. Iranians are generally Shiites, although other cultures might also have Shiites.

The Muslim Empire

In the precolonial era, powerful Muslim empires dominated the Middle East and North Africa and challenged European hegemony. The European colonial incursion into the region began in the 19th century and continued well after World War I. Even though Middle Eastern and North African countries have since gained independence, the region, in many ways, still remains dependent on Europe and the United States. This dependence has not gone unchallenged. Some say that the protracted Arab-Israeli conflict, the Iranian revolution, and the current problems in Lebanon and Iraq are all reflections of deep-seated resentments that have their origin in the colonial system.

Immigration to the United States

The first wave of Muslim immigration to this country lasted from the late 19th century until the 1920s, when restrictive legislation assigned small quotas to Middle Eastern countries. These early immigrants, primarily young men from the Middle East, were of humble origins and initially had no intention of settling in America. Eventually, Muslims began to settle in the country (primarily on the East Coast) and to establish permanent businesses such as small groceries, coffee houses and restaurants. The next step was social organization and, by 1952, there were more than 20 mosques making up the Federation of Islamic Associations of America.

The 1965 revision to U.S. immigration laws altered the quota system and allowed for a second wave of Muslim immigration. Several events have acted as "push" factors encouraging this emigration: the 1967 and 1973 Arab-Israeli wars, the 1975 Lebanese civil war, the 1978-79 Iranian revolution and the consolidation of the Islamic Republic of Iran, and the wars in Iraq. This new group of immigrants is far more diverse in terms of national and socioeconomic origins than those from earlier waves. These recent groups have tended to be more educated and professionally oriented.

Earlier groups of Muslim immigrants tended to settle on the East Coast. More recent Muslim immigrants have begun to go to such places as Southern California. There is a high rate of self-employment among Muslim groups. Many are highly skilled entrepreneurs such as doctors and dentists. For example, almost half of Middle Eastern men were working in managerial and professional jobs in 1990.

Be aware that not all Arabs are Muslim. While most Arabs are Muslim, the majority of Arab Americans are Christian.

With the Persian Gulf War, the events of September 11, 2001, and the current conflicts in Iraq and Afghanistan, many Muslims have been subjected to discrimination and negative stereotypes. It is important for sales associates to understand this fact and to let their Muslim clients know directly or indirectly that they are sensitive to their experience and are supportive of them.

The Muslim Market

In some major markets, such as Southern California, Muslims tend to cluster along cultural, ethnic and linguistic lines—at times emphasizing these characteristics over the unifying tenet of faith. In fact, it might be difficult for some to separate Islamic tenets from cultural traditions.

Surprisingly, African Americans make up more than 40 percent of the U.S. Muslim population (although some Muslims groups don't consider some predominately African American groups, like the Nation of Islam, to be true Muslims). South Asian groups—those of Indian/Pakistani, Bangladeshi, Sri Lankan or Afghani descent—make up almost a quarter of the Muslim population. Arab groups, or people from Arabic-speaking countries of the Middle East and North Africa, are about 12 percent of the population. Other African groups make up about 5 percent. Iranian Muslims, people of Persian descent usually from Iran, are around 4 percent of the population. Please note that Iranians are not considered to be Arabs. Turks compose about 2.5 percent, Southeast Asians (those from Thailand, Malaysia, Indonesia, Indochina or the Philippines) compose around 2 percent, and American Whites are approximately 1.5 percent of the Muslim population.

Some cultural groups are much more observant and conservative in their practice of Islam than others. Saudis are especially known for their religious conservatism. A person of another culture might not feel comfortable attending a Saudi-run mosque.

Degree of Acculturation

Muslim groups in America are constantly faced with problems concerning the maintenance of their cultural and religious heritage. Children of immigrants are subject to intense peer pressure from non-Muslim counterparts and often succumb to the pressures of Western society. For example, Muslim adolescents are pressured to participate in typical teenage behaviors like dating. Traditional Muslims object to U.S. courtship rituals of this type, which are often associated with premarital sex. Women are expected to remain pure until marriage and, theoretically, men are expected to do the same. Women who choose to dress in a more traditional manner are often faced with close scrutiny, suspicion and criticism. However, complete assimilation is often resisted. This can be attributed to several factors. One is national pride. This is especially true for Iranian immigrants. Another is residential patterns. Iranian groups, while residentially concentrated among native Whites, still live in close proximity to relatives, friends and other co-ethnics. Arabs, on the other hand, because of their tremendous heterogeneity, are much more scattered. Muslim immigrant groups are highly likely to marry within the group. Although intermarriage is more common in later generations, Muslim doctrine encourages marriage within the faith.

Economic Status

Approximately half the male population of foreign-born Muslim groups has a college degree, and more than half are involved in white-collar occupations. Almost all of the top 10 Middle Eastern vocational niches are managerial, professional and sales occupations. Physicians are among the top 10 occupational niches for both Iranian and Arab groups.

Holidays and Celebrations

Be aware that the Islamic calendar consists of 12 lunar-based months. Because lunar months are 29 or 30 days long, a year has 354 or 355 days, 10 or 11 days shorter than the solar year. Therefore, dates will change every year.

New Year (*Hijrah*): *Hijrah* means "migration" and refers to the Prophet's migration from Mecca to Madinah. The journey took place in 622 and marks the beginning of the Muslim calendar.

Ramadan: *Ramadan* is the ninth month of the Islamic year and is known as the month of fasting. During *Ramadan* there is no eating, drinking or sexual activity between dawn and sunset. (People physically unable to fast, such as the sick and those on a difficult journey, are excluded). After sunset, Muslims eat, drink and carry on normally. If possible, some Muslims take time off from their work for the last 10 days of *Ramadan* to isolate themselves from worldly affairs.

Eid al-Fitr: The first day of the month following *Ramadan* is *Eid al-Fitr*. This is the celebration of breaking the fast and is celebrated with special prayers, festivities and giving charity to the poor. This is a major holiday for Muslims. On this day, they visit relatives and friends and give gifts to their children.

Eid al-Adha: *Eid al-Adha* is the "Feast of Sacrifice" and is the second-most important celebration of Islam. It commemorates Abraham's willingness to sacrifice his son in obedience to God. It also marks the last and biggest day of the annual *Hajj*, or pilgrimage, to Mecca. Best clothes are worn and special prayers are said in the morning. Friends visit each other's homes, children receive presents and many families visit their ancestors' graves. Traditionally, the day begins with the sacrifice of an animal in commemoration of Abraham's sacrifice. The meat is then shared with the poor and with neighbors and friends. The holiday might be celebrated for three to four days, and Muslim businesspeople might or might not take days off for the celebration.

NOTES

Puerto Rican Americans

Puerto Rican Americans
SUMMARY

Demographics

- The Puerto Rican population of the United States increased 39 percent since 1990, from 2.7 million to 3.8 million in 2005.

Cultural Insights

- Puerto Rican worldview is largely based in a history of struggle and the present-day importance of freedom and self-expression.
- Self-identity is largely centered on a person's place in the family, his/her position in the social system and his/her performance in the group.
- Puerto Ricans usually converse at closer distance than North Americans.
- Most Puerto Ricans in the United States are able to speak English very well.
- For many of the unacculturated, punctuality is not a high priority.
- While independence is a core value among Anglos, interdependence is at the foundation of Puerto Rican norms and values.

Business Practices: Dos and Don'ts

Dos

- Personal relationships are often important in business dealings. Spend time forming a friendship before jumping into business discussions.
- If possible, when dealing with the unacculturated, print business cards with English on one side and Spanish on the other.

Don'ts

- A common misperception is that all Latinos are Mexican, especially in places such as California. Be careful not to refer to people from Puerto Rico as Mexican.
- Avoid usage of racial categories that are common in the United States. A darker-skinned Puerto Rican might not consider himself Black, as would a North American person of the same skin tone. In fact, Puerto Ricans in the United States resist being classified as Black or White.
- The pace of business negotiations can be much slower.
- Avoid frank criticism or any behavior that would demean another person in public.

Puerto Rican Americans

Demographics

According to the 2005 Census, between 1990 and 2005, the Puerto Rican population of the United States increased 39 percent. During that 15 years, the number of Puerto Ricans grew from 2.7 million to 3.8 million.

The 10 most Puerto Rican populated states (except Puerto Rico) in 2005 were:

1. New York (1,057,423)
2. Florida (645,240)
3. New Jersey (388,283)
4. Pennsylvania (260,580)
5. Massachusetts (217,347)
6. Connecticut (204,616)
7. Illinois (174,770)
8. California (147,076)
9. Texas (87,534)
10. Ohio (74,348)

The largest Puerto Rican markets in 2005 were in the following metropolitan areas:

1. New York (948,394)
2. Chicago (157,892)
3. Philadelphia (115,837)
4. Newark, NJ (94,077)

The two largest Puerto Rican populations in 2005 were located in two New York counties: Bronx County (319,884) and Kings County (203,676).

Cultural Insights

Worldview

- Puerto Rican worldview stems from a history of struggle and the present-day importance of freedom and self-expression.

- Puerto Rican culture values a present-day orientation. Life is to be enjoyed.

Sense of Self

- Self-identity is largely centered on a person's place in the family, his/her position in the social system and his/her performance in the group.

- There is a great deal of pride in the history and culture of Puerto Rico.

Sense of Space

- Puerto Ricans usually converse at a closer distance than North Americans.

- There is a good deal more physical contact (e.g., touching the arm, shoulder and lapel.)

Communication Style

- Both men and women are known to shake hands firmly.

- Close male friends shake hands; men kiss close female friends; close female friends might kiss each other.

- The Spanish language provides forms of formal and non-formal address (different use of *usted* vs. *tu* for the pronoun you, polite and familiar commands, and the use of titles of respect before people's first names, such as *Don* or *Doña*). In non-formal settings, conversations between Spanish speakers are usually loud and fast when compared to similar English- language conversations in the United States.

Eye Contact

- For Puerto Ricans, maintaining eye contact is typically quite important. Looking away might project distrustfulness.

- Unacculturated Latinos also might avert their eyes in unpleasant or highly charged situations and confrontations.

Language

- For more than 400 years, Puerto Rico was a colony of Spain. In 1898, after the Spanish-American War, the island came under the control of the United States. During Spanish rule, the principal language was Spanish. When the U.S. assumed control, there were attempts to introduce English, but Spanish remained the official language. The recent political landscape in Puerto Rico is divided between those who want independence (complete self-government), or statehood (to become a full U.S. state) and those who want to maintain their current status as a commonwealth (Puerto Ricans have U.S. citizenship, are not subject to individual and corporate taxes, are not represented in Congress, cannot vote in presidential elections and are subject to the military draft). Of all the issues, language is perhaps the most important one, since it permeates political, economic, educational, social and cultural lives. The adherents of all schools of thought are in agreement that Spanish should be the language of Puerto Rico. Still, the fact remains that a certain amount of official and commercial business in Puerto Rico is conducted in English. More importantly, most of the large numbers of Puerto Ricans living in the mainland United States have learned English, either out of necessity or by choice. Thus, most Puerto Ricans in the United States are able to speak English well. Many who live in Puerto Rico are bilingual. The population, to some extent, is familiar and comfortable with U.S. culture via their exposure to U.S. media and business interests.

Time and Time Consciousness

- Even with the unacculturated, who do not place a high priority on punctuality, you are usually expected to be on time. An exception can be found in social interactions like late dinners or parties, where it might even be considered rude to arrive on time.

Values and Norms

- While independence is a core value among Anglos, interdependence is at the foundation of Puerto Rican norms and values. Reliance on family and community are often components of success and survival for many Puerto Ricans in the United States.

- Respect for family is critical within Puerto Rican culture. Elders are respected, and duty to the family is critical. Studies show that although there are significant differences in acculturation between first and second generations and that the degree of formality when dealing with elders is lessening, there is still much interaction among generations.

- *Familismo* has to do with the high degree of interpersonal bonding within the Puerto Rican family, resulting in greater identification with the group and dependence on the family. Recent studies also have demonstrated the importance of the nuclear and extended family as a source of social support. Latinos might "adopt" close friends as *compadres* and family members in the absence of blood ties.

- *Machismo* characterizes the male gender role in Latino society. It stresses virility, independence and physical strength. It supports the idea that women are subordinate and inferior to men. However, with more exposure to North American attitudes, this belief is being questioned.

- *Marianismo* has been characterized as the complement of *machismo*. *Marianismo* defines the role of the ideal woman, modeled after the Virgin Mary, as based on chastity, renunciation and sacredness, while reinforcing obedience.

- Ideologies of race are different in the United States and Puerto Rico. In the United States, color lines are rigid between Whites and non-Whites. Classification is not as clear-cut in Puerto Rico. While Blacks are generally stigmatized and Whites are generally accorded higher status, dark skin does not automatically assign one to a racial group. Classification can depend on other visible characteristics, such as the shape of the mouth, nose and hair texture. Socioeconomic variables, such as occupation and education, also can affect a person's racial identity. A brown-skinned person who is well-educated might be referred to as White, while the same colored person who is not well-educated is more likely to be called *mulatto* or *moreno*. This has some effect on immigrants to the United States, who might often be considered Black but resent this classification.

Business Practices: Dos and Don'ts

Dos

- Personal relationships are generally important in business. Spend time forming a friendship before jumping into business discussions. Initiating the conversation with an inquiry about family is usually customary.

- When dealing with the unacculturated, if possible, print business cards with English on one side and Spanish on the other.

Don'ts

- A common misperception is that all Latinos are Mexican, especially in places like California. Be careful not to refer to people from Puerto Rico as Mexican.

- Avoid usage of racial categories that are common in the United States. A darker-skinned Puerto Rican might not consider himself Black, as would a North American person of the same skin tone. In fact, Puerto Ricans in the United States resist being classified as Black or White.

- The pace of business negotiations can be much slower.

- Avoid frank criticism or any behavior that would demean another person in public.

Historical Background

The Taino Indians originally populated the island of Puerto Rico. The island of Boriken was "discovered" by Columbus in 1493, and conquered by Spain in 1509. The native population, enslaved and eventually destroyed, was replaced by African slaves. This mixture of people led to the diverse color spectrum and culture known today as Puerto Ricans or *Boriquas*.

Slavery on the island was abolished in 1873. While the island was granted autonomy in 1897, after the Spanish-American War in 1898, Puerto Rico was ceded to the United States. U.S. capital had a profound effect on the mostly rural society. Increasing numbers of peasants were forced into the cities, resulting in a great increase in urban unemployment.

The Jones Act of 1917 granted Puerto Ricans a type of citizenship; however it was not equivalent to constitutional citizenship. This partial citizenship, however, did not prevent the United States from drafting Puerto Ricans into the armed forces during World War I, or from recruiting Puerto Ricans to labor in defense industries during the time of war. The 1917 Jones Act gave the islanders U.S. citizenship along with the obligation of serving in the American armed forces. However, they still could not serve in Congress, or run for or vote for President. During World War II (1939-45), the island became a key U.S. military base. Naval bases were constructed in San Juan Harbor and on Culebra.

In 1951, Puerto Rican voters approved a U.S. law granting them the right to draft their own constitution and soon the island was proclaimed as the Commonwealth of Puerto Rico. Since then, separate political groups have formed—most either supporting commonwealth status or statehood. At the same time, there has been continued agitation (violent at times) for complete independence from the United States.

The dividing line between the island and the mainland is quite literally fluid and is crossed by frequent travel and intercultural exchange. Despite their U.S. citizenship, however, Puerto Ricans still lie on the margins of the United States, separated by distance, language, racial difference and their different civic rights and duties.

Immigration to the United States

Since Puerto Rico was annexed by the United States in 1898 and Puerto Ricans were granted partial citizenship by birth in 1917, Puerto Ricans in the mainland United States are not immigrants in the literal sense of the term. However, despite an absence of legal restrictions on immigration and the economic conditions on the island, migration to the United States began slowly.

The first wave of immigrants to the United States took place during the late 19th and early 20th centuries. Between 1915 and 1930, more than 50,000 Puerto Ricans came to the United States, especially to New York City. They were generally people from urban areas with some education and experience as industrial workers. They were a great resource for a city in need of abundant, cheap and disciplined labor.

The majority of Puerto Rican immigration to the United States has occurred since the end of World War II and is due to three principal causes. The first cause was the rapid industrialization and urbanization of the island. In the late 1940s, the U.S.-sponsored Operation Bootstrap increasingly industrialized the country by encouraging local business and industries to open factories in Puerto Rico. However, the program did not create enough jobs to keep up with their rapid population growth. The second cause of immigration was the fact that the barrier of the long journey by sea disappeared with inexpensive air travel. The third, impetus to leave the island, was heightened by labor recruiters who promised the Puerto Ricans a better life in the industrial north.

Religion

Puerto Ricans are predominantly Roman Catholic, although many only attend church on major holy days. Puerto Rican Catholics are known to practice standard Catholic funeral rites (at times with the use of photographs of the deceased), baptism rites, confirmation rites and marriage ceremonies.

A religion called *Santería*, which was practiced by the African slaves under the guise of the Roman Catholic Church, is also practiced by some Puerto Ricans. It has its own priests and rituals, including divination, animal sacrifices, music and dancing, and utilization of both African and Spanish cultural practices.

Espiritismo (Spiritism) attracts some Puerto Ricans. Brought to Puerto Rico from Europe during the mid-19th century, this belief system promotes the idea that there is a spirit world that interacts with humans and the spirits of the dead. Practices include reading tarot cards, using herbal remedies, and using mediums to contact the dead.

Protestantism is more prevalent among the middle class.

Other Christian sects have been attracting a significant number of people in the lower socioeconomic strata since the 1970s, specifically the Jehovah's Witnesses.

The Puerto Rican Market

Puerto Ricans are an integral part of the past, present and future of the United States. Puerto Ricans, like African Americans before them, continue to provide a crust that other immigrants build upon. While some immigrant groups come to the United States and begin to prosper after a generation or two, Puerto Rican economic growth has been relatively slow. Despite 100 years of colonization and the influx of millions to the United States and United States citizenship, Puerto Ricans continue to be among the poorest ethnic populations in the States.

Degree of Acculturation

The Puerto Rican culture has maintained itself in the United States and largely resisted blending into the North American mainstream. In many neighborhoods, *colmados* and *bodegas* still supply the sustenance to many Puerto Rican families, and news and entertainment comes from a number of Spanish-language television and radio stations. In many parts of New York City, one can go through life speaking little or no English.

While there are some among later generations who have greatly assimilated into mainstream culture, most maintain a strong consciousness of their Puerto Rican heritage. For example, Puerto Ricans born in New York or who immigrated as young children might refer to themselves as Neo or Nuyorican. (These terms are sometimes considered derogatory, but are often accepted with pride by Puerto Rican youth.) Some might use Philliricans, Bostonricans or even mainlandricans, depending on where they live. Another popular term is *Boriqua* (Bor-ee-kwa, sometimes spelled *Boricua*), an affectionate and proud word that Puerto Ricans often use to refer to themselves. It is derived from the indigenous name for Puerto Rico, Boriken, which means "Home of the Brave and Noble Lords". *Boriqua* translates as "Brave Lord".

As U.S. citizens, Puerto Ricans are able to travel back and forth as they please. Second-generation immigrants or first-generation immigrants who have been here for several years, however, often claim to have a dual identity. They are considered *gringos* in their native land and immigrants in this one.

Economic Status

The first generations of Puerto Rican immigrants were significantly represented in low-skill jobs. Men became employed as unskilled factory operatives and menial help in hotels and restaurants. Women worked as domestics and as seamstresses in the garment industry. Since then, Puerto Ricans have struggled with low-paying jobs, high unemployment rates and deteriorating housing.

As of 2005, 25.6 percent of Puerto Ricans were employed in managerial and professional specialty occupations (compared with 37.7 percent of non-Hispanic Whites). About 21.5 percent worked in sales and administrative support, and 45.3 percent worked in service and as skilled workers, farmers or manual laborers. Puerto Ricans are much more likely than non-Hispanic Whites to be unemployed. In 2005, 6.9 percent of Puerto Ricans were unemployed, while only 3.6 percent of non-Hispanic Whites shared that status.

Education is highly valued among the Puerto Rican population. This is evident in the fact that, since 1994, the number of Puerto Ricans who have a high school education or more has increased from 59.4 percent to 71.2 percent in 2005. However, this percentage with a high school education, is still below that of non-Hispanics, which is 87 percent. In 2005, 14.8 percent of

Puerto Ricans had a bachelor's degree or higher (compared with 29.2 percent non-Hispanics).

Holidays and Celebrations

Because Puerto Rico is part of the United States, Puerto Ricans celebrate U.S. holidays. Other celebrations pertinent to the Puerto Rican experience include:

Año Nuevo (New Year's Day)—Jan. 1: Traditional Western holiday.

Day of the Magi/Day of the Three Kings (*Día de los Santos Reyes/Magos*)—Jan. 6: Traditionally, it is this day when gifts are dispensed (as opposed to Christmas Day) to commemorate the day when the Magi presented gifts to Jesus of Nazareth. This day is celebrated differently among different Latino groups in the United States and is losing some of its significance with the increased focus on Christmas. It is mostly considered a day for the children to receive gifts and to celebrate.

Easter and *La Semana Santa* (Holy Week): Easter is one of the highest holy days of the year for Latino Catholics. It is celebrated nearly everywhere in Latin America and Spain with religious observances and various types of processions. *Semana Santa* begins with Palm Sunday (*El Domingo de Ramos*), includes Good Friday (*El Viernes Santo*) and ends with Easter (*La Pascua de Resurrección*). The week is meant to mark the triumphant entry of Jesus into Jerusalem, followed by his death and resurrection.

Puerto Rican Week—Beginning of June: In New York, one week at the beginning of June is declared Puerto Rican Week and coincides with the Puerto Rican Day Parade. Each year at this time, the City of New York officially designates a week for the appreciation of Puerto Rican culture and to recognize the vast contributions of the Puerto Rican community in the city.

Puerto Rican Day Parade—Second Sunday in June: The first Puerto Rican Day Parade was held in New York City in 1958, and about 10,000 people attended. Presently, the parade is the largest open-air cultural celebration in the Northeast with more than 3 million attending. It is known for its uproarious enthusiasm. Initially, the parade struggled to get media coverage until 1991. Puerto Ricans are split on the necessity of continuing the parade as an exclusive Puerto Rican event or adapting it to a Hispanic Day Parade that would include all Hispanics. In the late 1990s, Puerto Ricans in California began organizing a similar celebration in Montebello. At present, close to 100,000 Puerto Ricans attend this event.

Hispanic Heritage Month—Sept. 15-Oct. 15: A month designated by the U.S. government to celebrate and explore Latino history and influence in this country.

Christmas Eve (*Nochebuena*) and Christmas (*Navidad*)—Dec. 24-25: Christmas Eve (December 24) is widely observed. Dinner and festivities take place on this day, rather than on Dec. 25, as is traditional in the United States.

Quinceañeras: A *quinceañera*, or 15th-birthday celebration, is a rite of passage for young, Catholic Hispanic girls, and is growing in popularity in the United States. The roots of the ceremony are found in a combination of indigenous and Spanish customs, and it is meant to represent a girl's emergence into womanhood. Girls are required to attend a year of religion classes before the celebration, which usually begins with a Mass followed by a party. The celebration itself tends be extravagant, and can rival a wedding in nature. The girl will wear an elaborate dress that symbolizes femininity, a gold medallion that expresses her faith, a ring that represents her spiritual and communal responsibilities, and a crown that symbolizes her living a Christian life. She will have 14 maids of honor, or *damas* (one for each year of childhood), and each will have a male escort—all of whom will perform a symbolic dance for the occasion. These events can cost thousands of dollars, and friends and relatives will often help with the costs.

NOTES

Russian Americans

Russian Americans

SUMMARY

Demographics

- In 2005, the total number of people of Russian descent in the United States was 3,009,876.

Cultural Insights

- Unacculturated Russians are known to be cautious, conservative people who value security and stability. They often prefer to avoid risk when possible.
- Seventy years of life under communism have fostered an affinity for the group.
- For Russian Jews, who comprise a large percentage of Russian immigrants, education is highly important.
- In the United States, Russian family dynamics are moving from the patriarchal rigidity of the communist society to a more flexible consumer-oriented American style.
- When unacculturated Russians converse, they typically stand closer than Americans do.
- Handshakes are a common form of greeting, both on arrival and departure.
- Elderly people are respected. It is considered good manners to recognize them and spend some time with them if language problems do not interfere.
- Unacculturated non-Jewish Russians are often direct, sometimes to the extent of being brusque and discourteous by U.S. standards of behavior.
- Direct eye contact is important in interpersonal discussions.
- Russians have traditionally had a different concept of time than Americans. Communism reinforced a *laissez faire* approach to time. This is changing in the United States, and Russians currently tend to be more punctual.
- Family and friends are extremely important in Russian society.

Business Practices: Dos and Don'ts

Dos

- Be on time. Although less acculturated Russians might have a more relaxed sense of time, those who have been in the United States for a significant amount of time will be punctual.
- Dress conservatively unless you know for a fact that it is acceptable to wear casual clothing.
- Have refreshments available if you are hosting the meeting.

Don'ts

- Don't be in a hurry to complete your negotiations. Unacculturated Russians have a lot of patience and can outwait anxious Americans. Remember their proverb, "Don't hurry to reply, but hurry to listen."
- Don't compromise your proposed outcome. Know what you want and stick to it. Russians

view compromise as a weakness that doesn't belong in negotiations.

- Don't consider any final offers made during initial negotiations. They are only opening ploys and will get better as negotiations continue.
- Don't let appearances of prosperity fool you. Make sure that things are as legitimate as they seem.
- Never put your hands in your pockets, which is considered bad manners. Don't whistle indoors, which is said to cause bad luck.

Russian Americans

Demographics

According to the 2005 Census American Community Survey, the total number of people of Russian descent in the United States was 3,009,876.

The 10 most Russian populated states in 2005 were:

1. New York (484,775)
2. California (439,534)
3. Florida (245,843)
4. New Jersey (208,717)
5. Pennsylvania (201,353)

6. Illinois (135,928)
7. Massachusetts (117,626)
8. Maryland (83,435)
9. Ohio (75,037)
10. Washington (74,395)

The top Russian markets in the United States are (NA indicates that exact population figures are not available):

1. New York City (254,896)
2. Los Angeles (180,805) *
3. Boston (90,968) *
4. Chicago (76,160) *
5. Detroit/Ann Arbor (NA)
6. Newark, NJ (NA)

Includes surrounding cities.

Cultural Insights

Worldview

- The Russian history of living under a communist regime for 70 years, coupled with the subsequent disintegration of that regime, has shaped the worldview of the people from that part of the world. They are patient when dealing with bureaucratic entities and, with a little help, rapidly master the intricacies of American bureaucracy.

- In order to survive in Russia, an individual had to learn to use his/her wits. Unacculturated Russians are known to be honest, straightforward and hospitable in their personal relationships.

- The unacculturated are also known to be cautious, conservative people who value security and stability and prefer to avoid risk when possible.

Sense of Self

- Occupational identity is an important source for feelings of self-worth. Russians often feel that their job defines them.

- Because they had to learn to deal with a repressive, corrupt government in the former Soviet Union, Russians are often pessimistic and especially mistrustful of the government. After the fall of the Soviet Union, many of the reformists' promises did not materialize and there was a great upsurge in crime. As a result, Russians are resilient, sensitive and patient. At the same time, they are experts at dealing with government bureaucracy and when something goes wrong in a business or personal matter, they might attempt to manipulate their environment—not always by government standards.

- Seventy years of communal life have fostered an affinity for the group. Russians enjoy and prefer group activities, such as organized sports or group dating.

- For Russian Jews, education has always been important, as it was a valuable portable commodity that easily passed through international borders.

Sense of Space

- Less acculturated Russians like to stand closer during conversations than do mainstream Americans. Physical contact with strangers is acceptable. It is acceptable to show affection to friends and acquaintances. Men might kiss and hug each other, and women might hold hands when walking down the street.

- Handshakes are a common form of salutation, both on arrival and departure.

Communication Style

- The Communists eliminated many of the customary social formalities. Today Russians, especially non-Jewish Russians, are direct, sometimes to the extent of what others might judge as being brusque and discourteous. They can be assertive, and discussions can quickly evolve into shouting matches, but with no offense intended. Russian Jews tend to be less confrontational in their communication style.

- Compromise is sometimes viewed as a weakness.

- In the United States, as with the majority population, Russian use of the computer is widespread. Much of this consists of e-mails. Many Web sites have been established to facilitate communication between the Russians in the United States and family and friends in the former Soviet Union.

Eye Contact

- Direct eye contact is important in interpersonal discussions.

Language

- The USSR was a large and diverse country with many different languages. In its effort to rule that country, the government mandated that the Russian language be used in all official business interactions and transactions. The Russian language is taught in all schools.

- There are still more than 25 languages other than Russian spoken in Russia today. Russian, however, continues to be the official language of communication used in all governmental, educational, professional and economic areas.

- Education in Russia is universal, and almost all adult Russians who enter the United States are literate in their native language. U.S. cities with large Russian populations support Russian-language TV stations, radio stations and newspapers. Some of the older Russian Jews speak Yiddish, but because of Soviet prohibition, that language has not been passed on to the younger generations.

- The vast majority of Russians who come to the United States intend to make this country their permanent home. They realize the importance of learning English and enroll in English classes in large numbers. English is a difficult language for them because its alphabet is different and because of the lack of commonalities in grammar. Most people younger than 40 seem to be able to learn English readily. As is the case with all immigrant groups, the older generation has had difficulty learning English.

Time and Time Consciousness

- Traditionally, Russians have had a different concept of time than Americans. Communism reinforced a *laissez faire* approach to time. A worker could not be fired and there was no incentive for punctuality. Although Russians tend to be punctual and efficient for business meetings, this attitude often does not apply for social occasions. An American invited to a social engagement will ask if the arrival time is American time or Russian time. Russian time can mean one or two hours after the designated hour. Once the Russian guests arrive, time is taken for small talk, then refreshments, then more talk about family problems and then, finally, the meal.

Values and Norms

- Russians might feel a separation between themselves and the mainstream American community. They often find it difficult to interact on both social and business levels. There is a certain mistrust of Americans, who they perceive to be less direct and truthful. Many perceive Americans to be a colder people who do not develop the kinds of intimate friendships and relationships that Russians do. Many also feel that American social events can be boring and cold when compared to the more lively social occasions that take place within their community.

- Family and friends are extremely important in Russian society. They offer an invaluable support system and act as bulwarks against some of the risks and uncertainties faced in everyday life. Unacculturated Russians view themselves not as individuals but as members of a group—family, religious institution, neighborhood. Russians speak of "our" family, "our" church, "our" neighborhood—not "my" family, "my" church or "my" neighborhood.

- Babies and children are carefully nurtured. Infants are fed on demand, swaddled and held for most of the time. Because most parents work, grandparents do much of the child rearing.

- Elderly people are respected. It is good manners to recognize them and spend some time with them if language problems do not interfere.

- Food is an important part of family life. As with many other ethnicities, it symbolizes both nurturing and cultural identity. A visitor to a Russian home always will be offered a glass of tea and something to eat. The unacculturated hostess will not take "no" for an answer.

- Sexual restraint is encouraged. Traditionally, particularly for Russian Jews, adult children are expected to remain at home until marriage.

- Many immigrants were members of the intelligentsia in Russia and continue to be interested in painting, dancing, music, literature and the theater. Conversations at social evenings often include discussions of politics, philosophy, literature and the arts.

- Unacculturated Russians have a reputation for loving parties. They celebrate family rituals and events with lavish displays of food, alcohol, music and dancing.

- Russians immigrants often have been described as having an ironic sense of humor that has helped them deal with the trials and tribulations of life in a communist country.

Business Practices: Dos and Don'ts

Dos

- Be on time. Although less acculturated Russians might have a more relaxed sense of time, those who have been in the United States for a significant amount of time will be punctual.

- In business negotiations, make sure you have a clearly defined goal.

- Present the facts succinctly and accurately. Include appropriate technical details.

- Believe that once you sign a formal contract, it is final. Russians usually will not renegotiate a done deal.

- Remember that Russians are masters at the waiting game.

Don'ts

- Do not be in a hurry to make a sale. Russians value patience. Remember their proverb, "Don't hurry to reply, but hurry to listen."

- Do not be surprised if negotiations become emotional.

- Do not compromise what you set out to accomplish. Know what you want and stick to it.

190

Unacculturated Russians frequently view compromise as a weakness that does not belong in negotiations.

- Do not consider any final offers made during initial negotiations. They are only opening ploys and will get better as negotiations continue.

- Do not let appearances of prosperity fool you. Make sure that things are as legitimate as they seem.

- Do not put your hands in your pockets, which is considered bad manners. Don't whistle indoors, which is believed to bring bad luck.

Historical Background

As a result of the country's geographical position straddling Europe and Asia, Russia's history reflects both a collision and an amalgamation of Eastern and Western influences. At the same time that the Vikings were raiding the western coasts of Europe and the British Isles, Viking traders were exploring Russia. They set up trade routes, worked and fought with the local tribes, and established small settlements. The city-principality of Kiev, an important player in Russian history, was founded and ruled by the Vikings. In the 13th century, the Mongols (also known as the Tartars), came from Asia and brutally conquered the regions now known as Moscow and Kiev. They were cruel rulers who enslaved the Russians. Moscow finally liberated itself from Mongol rule in 1480.

Russia was bypassed by the European cultural revolutions started by the Renaissance and by the political, cultural, industrial and scientific revolutions that fostered the growth of a large European middle class. Until the early 19th century, Russian society remained mired in the Middle Ages, controlled by an autocratic aristocracy that depended on millions of serfs to keep their largely agricultural economy viable. Russia continued to be an autocratic empire, ruled by a hereditary monarch, the czar, whose word was law.

Orthodox Christianity arrived in Russia in 988, spread throughout the country and, eventually, became the state religion of Russia. In 1453, as a result of the fall of Constantinople, the Russian Orthodox Church lost its connection with the other Orthodox Christian movements and developed its own liturgy and customs. The state religion continued to be the Russian Orthodox Church, and members of other religions, like Jews, were frequently subjected to state-organized violence and persecution. These religious minorities had restrictions on where they could live and what occupations they could pursue.

In 1917, the Russian or Bolshevik Revolution began the seven decades of Communist rule. Pure communism is encapsulated in the following phrase: "From each according to their abilities, to each according to their needs." After the revolution, the group took precedence over the individual. What was good for the state was considered good for the individual. In actuality, however, Russians had merely exchanged one kind of aristocracy for another. The Communists attempted to drag their countrymen into the modern world by changing most of their basic institutions. Formal religious observances were abolished, and the official religion became atheism. The rule of the aristocracy was exchanged for the rule of the bureaucrats. The czar was replaced by Josef Stalin, the Russian Army became the Red Army, and the czar's secret police were succeeded by the OGPU, which later became the KGB.

The USSR was a totalitarian regime that suppressed dissent of any kind.

In 1991, the Soviet Union collapsed. Economic challenge and increased crime followed. This added impetus to a new wave of Russian immigrants.

Immigration to the United States

There were four previous waves of immigration to the United States.

The first wave occurred when fur traders began crossing the Bering Strait to Alaska in the mid-1700s. In addition to fur traders, small communities of Molokan and Old Orthodox Christians came to Alaska to avoid religious persecution in Russia. Russian migration to Alaska came to an end in 1867, when Alaska was sold to the United States.

Substantial migration from Russia began again and extended from 1880 to 1914. It consisted predominantly of Russian peasants and Russian Jews. In 1870, the Russian government embarked on a program to "Russianize" the country by making life difficult for ethnic and religious minorities, The czar stated that the purpose was to kill off one-third of the minority population, force one-third to migrate, and convert the remaining one-third to the Russian Orthodox Church. As a result, many Jews were living in abject poverty and barely surviving. By 1914, more than 3 million Russians had immigrated to the United States, more than half of them Jews.

A second wave of immigration occurred after the Bolshevik Revolution. Russia's state religion was atheism, and all forms of organized religion were abolished. People who continued to practice their religions were persecuted. Twenty thousand Russian Jews and Russian Christians from non-Russian Orthodox churches came to the United States as a result of that persecution.

The third wave occurred after the end of World War II, when approximately 30,000 Russian immigrants managed to make their way to the United States.

The fourth and largest immigrant wave began in the early 1970s, when "Refuseniks" began successfully to challenge the Russian system of religious and political oppression. The worldwide publicity they received helped to facilitate their emigration.

Between 1989 and 1991, the USSR collapsed but anti-Semitism and repression of other religious minorities continues to this day. Russia's transition from a communist system to a capitalist system has been chaotic, and most Russians have suffered severe economic hardships. As a result, Russian immigrants are continuing to come to the United States in large numbers.

Religion

The Russian Orthodox Church has been the state religion in Russia since 988. Over the centuries, the Orthodox Church maintained that its belief and worship contained the only truth and, therefore, there was no need for religious pluralism.

In late 1917 and early 1918, the Communist government confiscated most of the church's property and separated the church from both the state and the educational system. Monks and priests were evicted, and many monasteries and churches were destroyed or used for secular purposes. Many religious objects were defaced or obliterated.

A religious revival began in the late 1980s, and the thousand-year anniversary of Russian Orthodoxy was celebrated widely throughout the USSR. In 1990, new laws were passed that lifted the restrictions on religious communities.

Organized anti-Semitism has been a factor in Russian life for centuries. Pogroms were killing sprees perpetrated by local peasants and militias organized by the czarist government. This hatred of Jews, fostered in the Russian people during czarist days, continued throughout the communist era and still exists today. For this reason, the largest number of Russian immigrants to the United States are Jewish. As a result of the communist suppression of the Jewish religion, most Russian Jews know little about their religion. Their identity as Jews comes from their family culture and official identification as Jews reported on their internal Soviet passports.

Russian-Americans

Russian immigrant success is often related to their educational level in Russia, their age, the length of time they have been in the United States, and their ability to access services designed to help them adjust to and succeed in their new country.

According to the Census American Community Survey in 2005:
- Median annual household income was $65,021.
- 54.4 percent of Russian Americans were employed in management and professional occupations.
- 56 percent of adults older than 25 had four-year degrees.

Degree of Acculturation

The fourth and largest wave of immigration (1970s to 2000) was unique in that it consisted largely of the educated middle class: professionals, teachers, doctors, nurses, dentists, lawyers, engineers, scientists and technicians. The desire to assimilate into the American experience is strongest among those refugees younger than 50. They attend ESL (English as a Second Language) classes and American Citizenship classes while working two or three minimum-wage jobs. As their English improves, they upgrade their professional skills and gradually find jobs that enable them and their families to live in the American lifestyle of their dreams.

Approximately 25 percent of the fourth wave of Russian immigrants consisted of older retirees. They struggled with English acquisition and had difficulty in coping with their changed environment. These older people tended to cluster in more familiar ethnic Russian neighborhoods.

Economic Status

Many different industries have grown up to meet the varying needs of this 3-million-plus population. Some of the economic activities they are involved with are:

- Ethnic food markets, bakeries, restaurants, clothing stores and import/export companies.
- Russian/American bookstores, newspapers, radio stations, TV channels, cyber cafes, Web sites and movie theaters.
- Day-care facilities, nursing homes, funeral homes, car dealerships, garages and travel agencies.
- Building contractors, real-estate developers, real-estate agents and insurance agents.
- Lawyers, doctors, nurses, alternative medicine practitioners, medical and dental clinics, classes in English as a Second Language, banking, driver training, computer programming and repair, and religion.

Holidays and Celebrations

Russian Americans observe traditional American holidays as well as some of the following Russian holidays. Also note that many Russians are also Jewish and observe Jewish holidays.

New Year's Day—Jan. 1: This is a big day for visiting and gift giving.

Christmas December 25 and January 7: While Russian Orthodox Christians celebrate Christmas on January 7, many other Russians celebrate on December 25.

Women's Day—March 8: Traditionally, this is a day when men give women gifts, usually flowers. Husbands are supposed to do the housework and take care of the children. Most Russians in America no longer celebrate Women's Day and have replaced it with Valentine's Day.

Day of Laughs—April 1: Americans call it April Fools Day. Russians call it The Day of Laughs.

Christmas—Dec. 25: Many Russians will celebrate Christmas on both Dec. 25 and Jan. 7.

NOTES

Thai Americans

Thai Americans
SUMMARY

Demographics

- In 2005, the Thai population in the United States was 143,169. About one-third of all Thai immigrants lived in California (45,341), and 14 percent (19,856) had settled in Los Angeles County.

Cultural Insights

- Unacculturated Thai Americans tend to be polite and guarded. Sparing another's feelings and not causing them to lose face is considered more important than factual truth. Many Thais alter their behavior in the United States, especially when dealing with non-Asian counterparts.
- Understand that unacculturated Thai Americans avoid confrontation at all costs. They will never say "no" but will, instead, make implausible excuses or pretend that they don't understand English. Likewise, they find it difficult to accept a direct negative answer.
- Although unacculterated Thais are getting more used to Western forms of expression, you will lose their respect if you express strong emotions. An unacculturated Thai will not show anger, disappointment or disgust to another person except in extreme situations.
- Bragging is frowned upon, as it demonstrates an empty soul.
- Moderation and caution in speech are motivated by an awareness of the danger that verbal excess can bring by creating discord and animosity. Because of this cultural predisposition, Thai Americans often appear to be reserved, nonresponsive or nonassertive by American standards.
- Important Thai holidays include the Lunar New Year, *Makha Puja* Day, *Songkran* Day and *Wisakha Puja* Day.

Business Practices: Dos and Don ts

Dos

- Be patient and flexible in your business dealings. Recognize that unacculturated Thais do not follow the same relentless work schedule that other cultures do. Allow sufficient time to reach your goal.
- Your initial meeting with unacculturated Thai American businesspeople might be over lunch or drinks so that they can get to know you. Do not, however, expect to discuss business at that time.

Don'ts

- Never lose control of your emotions and don't be overly assertive, as such behavior is considered poor manners. Also, you should never raise your voice, lose patience or get angry, as these are seen as weaknesses. Remember, Thai Americans strive for harmony.

- Never touch a Thai on the head, even in an act of affection or friendship. This is considered highly offensive.
- The feet are considered the lowest and dirtiest part of the body, so never point at anyone or anything with the soles of your feet.

Thai Americans

Demographics

According to the 2005 Census American Community Survey, the total number of people of Thai ancestry in the United States was 143,169.

About one-third (45,341) of all Thai immigrants lived in California, and 19,856 (13.9 percent) had settled in Los Angeles county.

The 10 most Thai populated states in 2005 were:

1. California (45,341)
2. Texas (10,651)
3. New York (8,107)
4. Florida (6,281)
5. Illinois (6,730)

6. Virginia (5,773)
7. Washington (5,508)
8. Nevada (4,003)
9. Maryland (3,457)
10. Massachusetts (3,044)

Cultural Insights

Worldview

- Thai culture, like other Asian cultures, is rooted in a strong sense of family. The Buddhist religion is also a major influence in Thai culture, as well as in the arts.

Sense of Self

- Politeness and the demonstration of respect are emphasized in Thai culture. Unacculturated Thais strive to maintain harmony with their family and friends.

Sense of Space

- Like Korean Americans and Japanese Americans, in social and business interactions, Thai Americans require more space than the general population.

Communication Style

- Unacculterated Thais tend to be polite and guarded. Sparing another's feelings is considered more important than factual truth. Many alter these practices in the United States, especially when dealing with non-Asian counterparts.

- Understand that Thais are known for avoiding confrontation at all costs. The unacculturated will never say "no", but will, instead, make implausible excuses or pretend that they don't understand English. Likewise, they find it difficult to accept a direct negative answer.

Eye Contact

- Direct eye contact is not the norm in Thai culture.

Language

- Thailand's national language is called Thai. Scholars believe that Thai is a form of Chinese that was gradually brought to the area between the 7th and 13th centuries. Within Thailand, there are actually several different Thai languages, but the one used by the government, schools and the media is the language known as Central Thai.

- Thai, like Mandarin and Cantonese, is a tonal language with five tones: high, middle, low, rising, and falling. Each syllable of a Thai word must be pronounced correctly and vocalized at a certain pitch. If the pitch is different, the word might have another meaning. For example, the word pronounced "my" can be said in five different tones, each producing a different meaning. "My" said in a high tone means "wood", and "my" said in a low tone means "new". These tonal differences make Thai a difficult language for foreigners to learn.

- Politeness and signs of respect are characteristics of the Thai culture and language. This is demonstrated by something called *kreng jai*, a term denoting respect for the status and hierarchy of others and a general approach toward others characterized by humility.

Time and Time Consciousness

- For Thais, punctuality is a sign of courtesy.

Values and Norms

- Part of the Thai nonconfrontational culture is never to lose face or cause others to lose face. Although Thai Americans are getting more used to Western forms of expression, you will lose their respect if you ever exhibit strong emotional reactions. An unacculturated Thai typically will not show anger, disappointment or disgust to another person except in the most extreme situations.

- For Thais, bragging is looked down upon, as it reflects an empty soul. Moderation and caution in speech are motivated by an awareness of the danger that verbal excess can bring by creating discord and animosity. Because of this cultural predisposition, unacculturated Thais often appear to be reserved, nonresponsive or nonassertive by American standards.

Business Practices: Dos and Don'ts

Dos

- Be patient and flexible in your business dealings. Recognize that Thais do not follow the same relentless work schedule that other cultures do. Allow sufficient time to reach your goal.

- Your initial meeting with Thai businesspeople might be over lunch or drinks so that they can get to know you. Do not, however, expect to discuss business at that time.

Don'ts

- Never lose control of your emotions. Don't be overly assertive. That is considered poor manners.

- You should never raise your voice, lose your patience or get angry, as these are seen as weaknesses and a lack of control. This behavior will get you nowhere. Remember Thais strive for harmony between all people and things.

- Never touch a Thai on the head, even in an act of affection or friendship, as it is considered highly offensive. Thais consider the head the most sacred part of the body and as home to a person's spirit, which protects their health.

- The feet are considered the lowest and dirtiest part of the body, so avoid showing the soles of your feet to others.

Historical Background

Thai history dates back to the 12th century and the monks who lived in what is now known as central Thailand. When these monks immigrated from the Indian subcontinent, they brought with them Buddhist culture. Thai culture is actually a combination of the influence of:

- The Sumatran-based Srivijaya culture from the north.
- The Khmer culture from the east.
- Influences from what is now southern China.

Thai princes formed the first Siamese capital in Sukhothai, and later in Chiang Mai and Ayutthaya. Prior to adopting the name Thailand, the nation was known to the world as the Kingdom of Siam.

During the 16th and 18th centuries, the Burmese attacked Siam, destroying Ayutthaya and seizing Chiang Mai. When Thais managed to drive away the Burmese, they moved the capital to Thonburi. In 1782, the current Chakri dynasty was formed by King Rama I, and the capital of Siam was moved across the Chao Phrya River to Bangkok.

Throughout the 19th century, Siam remained independent by cleverly playing off one European power against another. In 1932, a peaceful coup converted the country into a constitutional monarchy and in 1939, Siam became Thailand under King Ananda Mahidol.

Immigration to the United States

Most Thai Americans are part of an Asian-American immigration wave that peaked during the 1960s and 1970s. This was primarily due to the Immigration Act of 1965, which was fully implemented in 1968. Earlier, in 1952, Congress passed the McCarran-Walter Act to nullify the racial restriction of a 1790 naturalization act that specified that only White people could become U.S. citizens. Although the McCarran-Walter Act allowed non-Caucasians to be naturalized, it restricted the number of immigrants by a quota based on national origin.

Under President Lyndon B. Johnson's leadership and impacted by the growing Civil Rights consciousness of that era, Congress passed the Immigration Act of 1965 to amend the McCarran-Walter Act. The new law eliminated national-origin quotas and provided a legal framework within which increasing numbers of Thais immigrated to the United States.

While the Immigration Act of 1965 repealed the quota system, it introduced seven preferences for immigrants from countries in the eastern hemisphere. They include preferences for professionals, scientists and artists of "exceptional ability", and for skilled and unskilled workers in occupations in short supply in the United States. Thus, a large number of Thai professionals especially medical doctors, nurses, scientists, pharmacists and engineers immigrated between 1968 and 1976, creating a so-called "brain drain crisis" in Thailand. These professionals also brought with them their immediate families, siblings and parents.

Sociopolitical and economic conditions in Thailand during the late 1960s and 1970s also played a crucial role in this immigration pattern. The worldwide petroleum crisis had a significant impact on Thailand's economy, creating high inflation and job scarcity. Medical doctors, nurses, scientists and engineers were not paid at the rate they felt their special training deserved. Chances for professional development and mobility appeared to be limited. The country was under a military dictatorship and there was unrest among students, workers and farmers. In addition, the Vietnam War and wars in neighboring Laos and Cambodia threatened Thailand's security and stability, further driving immigration.

Thais who arrived in the United States under the Immigration Act of 1965 mainly settled in California, Texas, Illinois and New York. Because of their culture's emphasis on close ties to family and community, most Thai Americans chose to live near relatives and friends. Thus, they created ethnic residential communities such as those in Hollywood, California, and Elmhurst and Queens in New York City.

Religion

More than 95 percent of Thai Americans are Buddhists who belong to the Hinayana or Theravada sects. Animism, or spirit worship, and Hindu beliefs are liberally intertwined with Buddhism in Thai culture, as are the use of astrology and fortune telling.

Thai Americans

Many Thai American immigrants in the late 1970s and 1980s were young professionals, particularly doctors, nurses, white-collar workers and students. Spouses of U.S. military personnel contributed to the growth of the Thai American community.

Thai American restaurants are the most visible sign of the rapidly growing Thai population. Ranging from the elegant to the economical, Thai restaurants are increasingly popular in urban centers throughout the United States.

Holidays and Celebrations

Thailand is the only country in the world that observes the New Year three times. Thai people

204

celebrate the major American holidays as well as their own traditional celebrations. Despite the fact that most Thai are Buddhists, Thai children living in this country also enjoy taking part in Christmas activities.

New Year's Day—Jan. 1: Celebrations for the start of the New Year.

Lunar New Year's Day : There are many Thai Americans who have at least some Chinese blood, so this holiday is widely celebrated.

Makha Puja Day: The full moon of the third lunar month marks the occasion when 1,250 of the Buddha's disciples came to hear him preach. This day is a public holiday.

Songkran Festival (Thai New Year): In spring, everyone celebrates the traditional Thai New Year. The first day of the festival is *Maha Songkran* Day, which marks the end of the old year. The following day is *Wan Nao*, and the third day (on which the New Year begins) is *Wan Thaloeng Sok*. The festival is also known as the Water Festival, because it is believed that water washes away bad luck. In every home, images of Buddha are washed with rose-scented water. People also pay respects to their elders by pouring a little water over their hands. Outside, people go a little wilder and buckets of water are thrown over everything that moves.

Wisakha Puja Day: The full moon of the sixth lunar month is the most important date on the Buddhist religious calendar. It celebrates the Buddha's birth, enlightenment and death. Every year on this day, teachers in Thailand take part in a candlelight procession around the main chapel of a local temple. Flowers, three incense sticks and a lighted candle are taken to the temple. Worshippers walk around the chapel three times in a clockwise direction. Afterward, they listen to a sermon from a Buddhist monk.

NOTES

Vietnamese Americans

Vietnamese Americans
SUMMARY

Demographics

- Between 1990 and 2005, the Vietnamese American community grew at a substantial rate of 131 percent. The Vietnamese population in the United States increased from 614,547 in 1990 to 1,418,334 in 2005, or 8.7 percent a year.
- The largest Vietnamese markets are in Los Angeles and San Jose, California.

Cultural Insights

- The Vietnamese worldview bears the deep imprint of the various religions in the country.
- The Buddhist influence can be seen in the view of life on Earth as something transient and unstable.
- Confucian influence is manifested in a respect for education, family and elders.
- Taoism's imprint can be seen in the desire to avoid conflict.
- Respect is important in communication with any Vietnamese. It is expressed in the form of courtesy and in the effort to spare others from the humiliation of losing face.
- Vietnamese feel that a refined, well-mannered person is moderate, modest and moral, and demonstrates self-control.
- The most important Vietnamese American holidays are *Tet* (usually in February), *Trung Nguyen* (usually in August) and *Trung Thu* (usually in September).

Business Practices: Dos and Don'ts

Dos

- Unlike in Vietnam, shaking hands is acceptable in business and social settings in the United States. However, if you are a female dealing with a male, you should be sensitive to your clients. How do they greet you? Do they offer to shake hands? If they do, by all means reciprocate. If they do not, and you attempt to shake hands and they appear resistant, do not take it personally.
- When talking, crossing your arms is a form of respect. In Vietnam, there is a passive pose for crossing your arms (similar to cradling a baby); it is not the interlocking of the arms as in the West, which is seen as defiant.
- Vietnamese culture is concerned more with status (obtained with age and education) than with wealth. *Thua* (meaning "please") is added in front of the first name to show respect. To show respect, unacculturated Vietnamese will bow their heads to a superior or elder.
- Always follow through with promises.
- Refer to other Vietnamese you have spoken with.
- When in doubt, dress conservatively.

Don'ts

- Don't assume that your potential client/customer speaks or prefers to speak Vietnamese.

- Don't use his/her first name until you have established a relationship.
- Do not put your hands in your pockets when conversing. This is disrespectful and emits cockiness.
- Most Vietnamese will not speak loudly in the presence of others. They believe speaking softly is an indication of humility.
- Do not pat a person on the back, especially if the person is older or of a higher rank. You can do this only with close personal friends.
- Do not point at other people when talking. It is disrespectful.
- Vietnamese are known for being modest and for deflecting laudatory comments. Profuse praise can be regarded as mockery and also can be insulting. Insults to elders or ancestors are quite serious and often lead to severed social ties. Indirect praise is better than direct praise (e.g., "My hair could never look as good as yours," would be preferred instead of the direct "You have beautiful hair").

Vietnamese Americans

Demographics

The growth rate in the Vietnamese American community between 1990 and 2005 was substantial, at 131 percent. The Vietnamese American population grew from 614,547 in 1990 to 1,418,334 in 2005, or 8.7 percent a year.

In 2005, the 10 most Vietnamese populated states were:

1. California (539,150)
2. Texas (159,107)
3. Washington (60,543)
4. Florida (55,555)
5. Washington DC (42,610)
6. Virginia (48,035)
7. New York (39,131)
8. Georgia (37,159)
9. Pennsylvania (35,111)
10. Oregon (25,684)

In 2005, the top 10 Vietnamese regional markets in the United States were:

1. Orange County, CA (157,012)
2. Santa Clara County CA (106,893)
3. Los Angeles County (103,332)
4. Houston (77,364)
5. Washington DC (42,610)
6. San Diego (38,514)
7. Dallas (32,637)
8. Seattle/Tacoma (29,952)
9. Sacramento County CA (24,315)
10. Alameda County CA (23,659)

Cultural Insights

Please note that much of what we are presenting here reflects a traditional view of Vietnamese culture. Since moving to the United States in large numbers, Vietnamese people and their culture continue to change. This change reflects the synthesis between traditional culture and the demands and the experience of life in the United States.

Worldview

- Many Vietnamese customs are rooted in both the Confucian respect for education, family and elders, and the Taoist desire to avoid conflict.

- The Vietnamese philosophy of life bears the deep imprint of the various religions in the country. For example, the Buddhist influence can be discerned in the view of life on Earth as something transient and unstable. The Vietnamese are known for a stoic approach toward life characterized by the acceptance of their circumstances, regardless of the situation.

- The family is the basic institution in Vietnamese life. It perpetuates society and protects the individual. Vietnamese family structure is more complex than that of Americans, which is essentially nuclear in nature and excludes relatives and in-laws. In the

Vietnamese family, roles are more numerous and more defined than in its American counterpart, and participation by members of the extended family is more common.

- Each member of the extended family has a title; for example, a father's third-youngest sister would be addressed as "third aunt", not by her given name. Older relatives are called by their title, but sometimes younger relatives are called by their given name. Also, it is common to see two or three generations of Vietnamese living in the same household. After marriage, Vietnamese women traditionally retain their own last names. Having a male child is often viewed as a great honor among the Vietnamese.

- Although historically Vietnamese are known for having a peaceful demeanor, because of the threats they have had to endure they also have become known for reacting vigorously in the face of adversity.

Sense of Self

- Most things a Vietnamese individual does, he/she does out of consideration for the welfare of the family and others, rather than for himself/herself alone.

- Bragging reflects an empty soul. Moderation and caution in speech are motivated by an awareness of the danger that verbal excess can bring by creating discord and animosity. Because of this cultural predisposition, the Vietnamese often erroneously appear to be reserved, nonresponsive or nonassertive by American standards.

- Vietnamese tend to be polite and guarded. Sparing another's feelings is considered more important than factual truth. As they acculturate to life in the United States, Vietnamese alter these practices, especially when dealing with non-Asian people.

Sense of Space

- The overarching theme in social interactions is the supremacy of respect. Vietnamese are, therefore, thoughtful in social interactions. This dictates maintaining a sense of space.

- There is a defined line of space that should be maintained between members of the opposite sex—usually about a foot in distance. This standard also applies for interactions between people of different ages.

Communication Style

- Respect is central to the Vietnamese communication style and is expressed in the form of courtesy and in the effort to spare others from the humiliation of losing face. Maintaining face is extremely important for the Vietnamese. The individual who loses face will have to endure public ridicule in the midst of his/her community. Furthermore, the family shares any social disgrace that is incurred.

- To avoid confrontation or disrespect, many Vietnamese will not vocalize disagreement. Instead of relaying negative communication, they might not answer a question. Moreover, you might experience an individual saying "yes" in a conversation even though they mean "no", or might not understand what you are saying.

- For certain feelings, Vietnamese culture prefers nonverbal communication, while American culture is more inclined to use words. For casual and informal circumstances, feelings of gratitude (thank you) or apology (I'm sorry) are not expressed verbally, but by nonverbal expressions, such as with silence or a smile.

- Moderation and caution in speech constitutes a distinctive feature of Vietnamese culture. From childhood, a Vietnamese is taught to think deeply before opening his/her mouth. In the words of a well-known Vietnamese proverb, "To open his mouth only when asked to and to answer only when beckoned to." This attitude is, in part, prompted by the belief that wise and talented people are modest in action and speech. Vietnamese value listening. According to the Vietnamese, good children praise their parents, and children show their respect by not speaking until spoken to. By conforming to this norm, a child brings pride to the family.

Eye Contact

- When talking, one should not look steadily at a respected person's eyes.

- In Vietnamese culture, looking into somebody's eyes, especially when this person is of a higher status (in age or social or family hierarchy) or of a different gender, usually means a challenge or an expression of deep passion. The proper respectful behavior is to avoid eye contact in talking to somebody who is not an equal or of the same sex.

Language

- Vietnamese has three basic dialects. Most Vietnamese speakers generally understand all of them. Vietnamese is basically a monosyllabic language having six tones, which give it a "singsong" effect. A word can be repeated with any of the six tones to indicate six different meanings. For example the word "ma" has six different meanings according to the tone that the word carries. This tonal quality is similar to Mandarin (which has six tones) and Cantonese (which has eight tones). It is very different from English. Verbs do not change forms; articles are not used; nouns do not have plural endings; there are no prefixes or suffixes; and there is no distinction among pronouns. The complex Vietnamese vocabulary reflects basic cultural values. For example, there are two forms of the verb "to eat," and usage is determined according to whether the people involved are of higher or lower status.

- Many Vietnamese refugees who moved to the United States during the first wave of immigration are bilingual. Older, urban Vietnamese might speak some French. Among the older population, those who had governmental jobs in South Vietnam speak some English, some of them fluently.

- When engaging in conversation, the Vietnamese are mostly aware of respect factors, such as utilization of full sentences. For example, a solitary, "Yes," as an answer to a question, without specifying content (e.g., "Yes, I did go to the park earlier,") might be construed as disrespectful.

Time and Time Consciousness

- Generally, the Vietnamese have a more relaxed sense of time than other Asian cultures. Because most Vietnamese immigrants come from rural areas, their economy was based on the cycles of nature. Thus, they are not as attached to the Western concept of time. This principle does not necessarily apply to urban Vietnamese but, in general, time is not as rigid in comparison to Western standards.

Values and Norms

- Certain virtues seem to have a greater appeal to the Vietnamese than others. Most conspicuous are moderation, modesty, moral propriety and self-control. To most Vietnamese, these are qualities of a refined, well-mannered person.

- Vietnamese society respects age. The Vietnamese recognize that a long life is a sign of inner virtue and that the elders are the carriers of tradition and the embodiment of knowledge and wisdom. Old people enjoy high respect in Vietnamese society, irrespective of wealth, education or social position. This respect is expressed in both attitude and behavior. Unlike Western societies that put a premium on youth, Vietnamese society is proud of its elderly. Age is an asset, not a drawback.

- Diligent and intellectually lively, the Vietnamese normally show great respect for learning and scholars.

- With a long artistic tradition, the Vietnamese culture is remarkable for its crafts (bronze, lacquer, wood and ceramic works, and fine inlays). Most Vietnamese devote much of their time to the decoration of their homes. The societal value placed on art is particularly noticeable in the embellishments of tombs and pagodas.

Business Practices: Dos and Don'ts

Dos

- Provide perks when possible. Unacculturated Vietnamese are known to like deals and extras.

- Unlike in Vietnam, shaking hands is acceptable in social or business settings in the United States. However, if you are a female dealing with a male, you should be sensitive to your clients. How do they greet you? Do they offer to shake hands? If they do, by all means reciprocate. If they do not, and you attempt to shake hands and they appear resistant, do not take it personally.

- When talking, crossing your arms is a form of respect. In Vietnam, there is a passive pose for crossing your arms (similar to cradling a baby), it is not the interlocking of the arms as in the West, which is seen as defiant.

- Vietnamese culture is concerned more with status (obtained with age and education) than with wealth. *Thua* (meaning "please") is added in front of the first name to show respect. To show respect, unacculturated Vietnamese will bow their heads to a superior or elder.

- Always follow through with your promises. When possible, deliver more than what you promised.

- Refer to other local Vietnamese whom you have dealt with or know. It adds to your credibility by showing that you have experience in general—and specifically with the Vietnamese community—and that you know what your clients need.

- When in doubt, dress conservatively. You will have more credibility at the onset, especially if you're young.

Don'ts

- Don't assume that your Vietnamese customer speaks Vietnamese or prefers to speak Vietnamese. This might be perceived as insulting.

- Don't use your customer's first name until you have established a long-term relationship. Use titles (e.g., Dr.) to show respect.

- Don't repeatedly mispronounce names. This demonstrates you are not trying. Ask the client to help you pronounce his/her name correctly.

- Do not put your hands in your pockets when conversing. This is disrespectful and communicates an arrogant attitude.

- Because the Vietnamese believe humility is a value, never exaggerate your ability to deliver.

- Most unacculturated Vietnamese will not speak loudly in the presence of others. They believe speaking softly is an indication of humility.

- Do not pat a person on the back, especially if the person is older or of a higher rank. You can do this only with close personal friends.

- Do not point at other people when talking. It is disrespectful.

- Avoid direct praise. Most unacculturated Vietnamese are modest and deflect laudatory comments. Profuse praise can be regarded as mockery and also can be taken as an insult. Insults to elders or ancestors are quite serious and often lead to severed social ties. Indirect praise is better than direct praise (e.g., "My hair could never look as good as yours," would be preferred instead of the direct, "You have beautiful hair.")

Historical Background

Early History

The first Vietnamese brought their economy, based in rice farming, with them from China. Rice production requires complex irrigation and collective farming. This led to the development of a strong sense of community in Vietnamese villages. Their first recorded history begins in 208

B.C., when Trieu Da, a defiant Chinese general, established his own empire of Nam Viet, which included northern Vietnam. Later, in the first century B.C., the Han dynasty of China expanded and incorporated Nam Viet into the Chinese Empire as the province of Giao Chi. This was the beginning of a long Chinese occupation and domination.

Despite more than a millennium of Chinese occupation, the Vietnamese retained a strong and separate cultural identity. There were numerous revolts against the Chinese, but none was successful until the 10th century. That is when Emperor Dinh Bo Linh won Chinese recognition and was paid regular payments of tribute for his new nation. He called this new state Dai Co Viet (the Kingdom of the Watchful Hawk).

The Mekong Delta, which had been under Cambodian control, was seized in the 16th century by a southern Vietnamese clan that had been constantly fighting a clan to the north. This conflict divided Vietnam at about the 17th parallel.

Colonialism

In the mid-16th century, the Portuguese became the first Europeans to sail to Vietnam. Later, the Dutch and English established small trading centers. The Catholic Church—first via the Portuguese and later along with the French—won many converts among the Vietnamese, despite many emperors' efforts to eradicate the religion.

Significant French influence in Vietnam started during the 17th century. By the mid-19th century, the French had gained control of Vietnam. Throughout French occupation, there were pockets of Vietnamese resistance, but these efforts were not unified.

Under French rule, Vietnamese were second-class citizens. Many people were displaced from their lives as rice farmers and forced to work under horrible conditions in rubber plantations and coal mines. Though a Confucian system of education was well-established, this was replaced by a French system under which students had to read and write French (even though about 80 percent of the population was literate in Chinese). It was during this time that resistance to French occupation solidified, and a young man named Ho Chi Minh formulated his nationalistic ideals.

The Vietnam Conflict

In 1941, Ho Chi Minh formed the revolutionary Vietminh in northern Vietnam to fight both the French and Japanese for control of the country. When Japan surrendered to the Allies following WWII, Ho's Vietminh declared independence. This independence was brief, as the British soon landed in Saigon and returned authority to the French. While France was planning to reoccupy the north, Ho, violating a previous agreement with France, proclaimed a separate government for Vietnam. Fighting broke out in Hanoi. Ho then retreated to create a rural northern base for his revolution.

Subsequent to the French loss in the Battle of Dien Bien Phu, the 1954 Geneva Accord divided Vietnam along the 17th parallel into north and south. Soon, the United States was training the South Vietnamese army. In 1955, Ho began accepting Soviet aid in the North, heightening U.S. interest in and support for the South. In 1964, the U.S. Congress, passed the Tonkin Gulf

Resolution. This led to increased U.S. support for and presence in South Vietnam. Soon the Viet Cong (a Vietminh-backed communist group) attacked the South with guerrilla warfare. The United States continued to support South Vietnam and was drawn into the war. In 1973, with no permanent end in sight, the United States signed a cease-fire agreement and retreated. Communist forces took Saigon in 1975. The war was enormously destructive, with about 60,000 Americans, more than 1 million South Vietnamese, and between 500,000 and 1 million North Vietnamese all losing their lives.

Immigration to the United States

The Vietnamese people who worked with the U.S. government or who sympathized with the South feared for their lives once the Communists gained power. Thus, in 1975, 130,000 Vietnamese fled to the United States. This group of immigrants was mostly young, well-educated, English-speaking urban dwellers. Fifty-five percent were Catholic, and many were able to bring their families intact. Most were kept at relocation centers on U.S. military bases until sponsors were found to help them resettle. This is referred to as the first wave of immigrants.

The second wave of refugees (1976 to 1984) was a more diverse group. It included people with differing ethnicities, nationalities, religions and languages—including many Vietnamese Chinese. Most of this group were less educated, less literate (in Vietnamese or English), less familiar with Western norms and values, and more rural than those in the first wave.

A third wave of refugees arrived from 1985 to 1991 and continues to arrive in small numbers today. This group includes both Vietnamese and ethnic Chinese people brought to the United States through family reunification programs. Additionally, in 1988 and 1989, the U.S. government negotiated the release of political detainees held in "re-education" camps by the Communist government. Many people in this wave spent years in camps under devastating conditions.

Vietnamese immigrants who had lived in rural areas were less likely to speak languages other than Vietnamese. Some had difficulties learning to read and write a second language because as farmers, they were not literate even in their native Vietnamese.

Religion

Vietnam has a diversity of religions. The vast majority of Vietnamese consider themselves Buddhist. Foreigners, primarily French missionaries, introduced Christianity in the 17th century. One important feature about Vietnamese culture is its religious tolerance. The religious belief system of the typical Vietnamese is a synthesis of the three traditional religions (Buddhism, Confucianism and Taoism) that have been coexisting peacefully for centuries in Vietnam. In Buddhism, the focus is on compassion and perfecting one's life to reach enlightenment. Confucianism is a philosophical system of beliefs that focuses on the individual and relationships between individuals and their families, and between the individual and society. The institution of ancestor worship bears witness to the influence of Confucianism on Vietnamese culture, and reflects the profound desire of the Vietnamese to survive in the heart and memory of loved ones after they have gone to the world beyond. Vietnamese people of all faiths share ancestor worship. A primary tenet of Taoism is *Wu-Wei*, or "no action," which means to seek equilibrium in life.

The Vietnamese American Market

Vietnamese Americans tend to be educated. Twenty-six percent of Vietnamese-Americans have a bachelor's degree or higher. They have a very high incidence of preference for their native language.

Economic Status

In 2005, the median Vietnamese American household earned $50,925 and 65.5 percent lived in owner-occupied dwellings. The majority of Vietnamese Americans hold managerial, technical and professional positions.

Holidays and Celebrations

Tet (Vietnamese Lunar New Year celebration): This most important Vietnamese festivity of the whole year is celebrated an entire week from the first to the seventh of the New Year according to the traditional lunar calendar. As the celebration depends on the phases of the moon, not the sun, it is celebrated on different dates of the Western calendar. In Vietnam, *Tet* is like Christmas, New Year's and Thanksgiving combined. Traditionally, during the first three days of *Tet*, family members visit one another. Younger family members will visit older family members with gifts and good luck wishes. During this time, money will be put in red envelopes to be given out to family and friends as a symbol of good luck for the New Year. Because these days are considered an omen for the course of the entire year, the belief is that if you eat a great deal during *Tet*, there will be enough food during the whole year. Thus, a lot of food is consumed during these celebrations. Bad luck or sickness during *Tet* are indications that the year will be negative. Arguments are avoided at this time. Vietnamese also attempt to see the image of a dragon during these celebrations. In Asian culture, dragons are generally a positive symbol. They connote a connection to the divine.

1975 Commemoration: This date commemorates the communist conquest of South Vietnam, Cambodia and Laos in 1975. This day is celebrated as a national holiday in Vietnam. However, it is a solemn occasion for many Vietnamese Americans, who recall this time with sadness.

Buddha's Birthday: This holiday commemorates the birth, enlightenment and death of the Buddha. It generally falls in May.

Trung Nguyen (Day of the Wandering Souls): On this day, the souls of the dead are believed to wander to the habitats of their offspring. In addition to the celebrations that occur in Buddhist temples, many festivities occur in peoples' homes where particular areas are assigned for devotion to deceased relatives. Food is spread on altars for the souls of the deceased, and imitation money is burned in their honor. Imitation money is burned so that the smoke can rise to the heavens and the deceased relatives can use it. This is done to let relatives know that their kin are thinking of them. The date that this holiday is celebrated changes from year to year, as it is based on the lunar calendar.

Vu Lan Day/Le Vu Lan (Mother's Day): Traditionally, pious children set up an altar to the dead and give to the poor on Vietnamese Mother's Day.

218

Trung Thu (Mid-Autumn Festival): *Trung Thu* is an autumn celebration. Traditionally, children parade through the streets with lanterns. Moon cakes are baked for this celebration. *Trung Thu* is also based on the lunar cycle, so the date of its celebration varies. This is a family-oriented holiday, similar to Halloween in its pageantry. The family makes ornate lanterns—a craft that is passed down through the family from generation to generation.

Birthday of Confucius: Confucius is revered in Vietnamese society. It is important to remember the China borders Vietnam, and its culture has had a great impact on its neighbor to the south. Again, the date will fluctuate depending on the lunar calendar.

NOTES

Bibliography

BIBLIOGRAPHY

Ahmed, Akbar S. 1995. "Where the Normal American Meets the Muslim Cleric". New Perspectives Quarterly. 12:2 (Spring).

Andres, Thomas. 1981. *Understanding Filipino Values*. New Day Publishers.

Arkoff, Abe. 1959. "Need Patterns in Two Generations of Japanese Americans in Hawaii". Journal of Social Psychology: 50.

Bakalian, Anny P. 1992. *Armenian-Americans: From Being to Feeling Armenian*. New Brunswick: Transaction Publishers.

Basch, Linda G. et al., 1994. N*ations Unbound: Transnational Projects, Post-Colonial Predicaments and Deterritorialized Nation-States*. New York: Gordon and Breach.

Bernard, Nancy. 1993. "The Lecher, the Witch and the Weirdo: Mainstream Reporting of Alternative Religions". Neiman Reports. 47:2 (Summer).

Bloom, Leonard and Ruth Reimer. 1949. *Removal and Return: The Socio-Economic Effects of the War on Japanese Americans*. Berkeley: University of California Press.

Bonacich, Edna. 1989. "Inequality in America: The Failure of the American System for People of Color". Sociological Spectrum 9: 71-101.

Bonacich, Edna and J. Modell. 1981. *The Economic Basis of Ethnic Solidarity*. Berkeley: University of California Press.

Bond, Philip & Robert Townsend. 1996, July-August. "Formal and informal financing in a Chicago ethnic neighborhood". Economic Perspectives, 20 (4), 3-28.

Bozorgmehr, Mehdi et al. 1996. "Middle Easterners: A New Kind of Immigrant", in *Ethnic Los Angeles*. Roger Waldinger and Mehdi Bozorgmehr, eds. New York: Russel Sage.

Brandon, Karen. 1999, November 2. "Lack of Banks in Ethnic Neighborhoods Seen as Key Barrier for Minorities". Chicago Tribune.

Chan, Sucheng. 1991. *Asian Americans: An Interpretive History*. New York: Twayne.

Cheng, Lucy and Philip Q.Yang. 1996. "Asians: The 'Model Minority' Deconstructed", in *Ethnic Los Angeles*. Roger Waldinger and Mehdi Bozorgmehr, eds. New York: Russel Sage.

Ciment, James, ed. *Encyclopedia of American Immigration*. Sharp Reference.

Civil Rights Issues Facing Asian Americans in the 1990s. U.S. Commission on Civil Rights.

Coleman, Murray. 2001, January 8. "Chinese-Americans are Online". *Investor's Business Daily*.

"Cross-Cultural Marketing: Financial Firms Becoming More Savvy in Targeting Asian-Americans". 2000, March. *Financial Service Marketing*.

Daniels, Roger. 1990. *Coming to America*. New York: HarperCollins.

Deep, Said. 1995. "Rush to Judgment (blaming Muslims for terrorist attacks)". *Quill*. 83:6 (July-August).

DeGenova, Mary Kay. 1997. *Families in Cultural Context: Strengths and Challenges in Diversity*. Mountain View, California: Mayfield Publishing Company.

DeVoss, David. 2000, January 24. "Web Sites Eye Asian-American Market". *Investor's Business Daily*.

Edmonds, A. 1994. *Korea: A Cultural Resource Guide*. St. Louis, MO: Milliken Publishing Company.

Fadahunsi, Olayinka. 1997, June "Profiling the Black investor: a long neglected market begs to be tapped". Black Enterprise, 27 (11), 70.

Fast, J. and J. Richardson. 1979. *Roots of Dependency: Political and Economic Revolution in 19th Century Philippines*. Quezon City, Philippines: Foundation for Nationalist Studies.

Feagin, Joe R. and Melvin P. Sikes. 1995. *Living With Racism: The Black Middle Class Experience*. Boston: Beacon Press.

Feagin, Joe R. and Clairece Feagin. *Racial and Ethnic Relations*, 6th edition, 1999.

Feagin, Joe R. and Nancy Fujitaki. 1972. "On the Assimilation of Japanese Americans". *Amerasia Journal*: 1, pp. 15-17.

Francis, Bruce and Kathleen Hays. 2002. April 24. "Sin Free Stocks". CNNfn: *Markets Impact*.

Gardner, R. et al. 1985. "Asian Americans: Growth, Change and Diversity". *Population Bulletin*: 40: 5-7.

Gibson, David. 2000. "Jersey Gives its Blessing to Muslim Dietary Practices". *The Star Ledger*: June 18.

Glenn, E.N. 1986. *Issei, Nisei, War Bride: Three Generations of Japanese Women in Domestic Service*. Philadelphia: Temple University Press.

Gochenour, Theodore. 1990. *Considering Filipinos*. Yarmouth, Maine: Intercultural Press.

Granelli, James S. 1995, February 6. "Banking on Asian American Community". *Los Angeles Times*.

Grant, David et al. 1996. "African Americans: Social and Economic Bifurcation", in *Ethnic Los Angeles*. Roger Waldinger and Mehdi Bozorgmehr, eds. New York: Russel Sage.

Halperin, Jennifer. 2001. "Muslim Women Say They Find Liberation in Modest Attire". *The Columbus Dispatch*: May 19.

Hamilton, Denise. 1995, April 9. "Banking on the Family Name". *Los Angeles Times*.

Hernandez, Debra Gersh. 1994. "Religious Stereotyping by the Media". *Editor and Publisher*. 127:36 (Sept 3).

Hing, Bill Ong. 1993 *Making and Remaking Asian America Through Immigration Policy, 1850-1990*. Stanford, Ca: Stanford University Press.

Holt, B. 1956. *Seed from the East*. Los Angeles, CA: Oxford Press.

Hurh, W.M. 1998. *The Korean Americans*. Westport, CN: Greenwood Press.

Hussain, Rashad. 2001. "On the Muslim Question". *Harvard Political Review*, Spring 2001.

Ikehara, Akiko. 2001. *Personal Interview*. Max Song.

Jacobson, David. 1998. *The Immigration Reader*. Malden, Massachusetts: Blackwell Publishers.

Joint Center for Housing Studies, Harvard University. 2000. "State of the Nation's Housing: 2000". Retrieved on May 29, 2002 from the World Wide Web: www.jchs.harvard.edu/publications/markets/SON2000_ch3.pdf.

Kang, K. Connie. 1996, August 8. "They've Got Luck All Figured Out". *Los Angeles Times*.

Kangvalert, W. 1986. "Thai Physicians in the United States: Causes and Consequences of the Brain Drain". Ph.D. diss., State University of New York at Buffalo.

Karp, J. 1995. "Migrant Workers: A New Kind Of Here". *Far Eastern Economic Review* 158: 42-45.

"Keeping the Faith". 2002, May 1. *On Wall Street*.

Kelley, Ron. 1994. "Muslims in Los Angeles", in *Muslim Communities in North America*. Yvonne Yazback Haddad and Jane Idleman Smith, eds. Albany: State University of New York.

Kim, K.Y. 1996. "Funeral Customs of Korea".

Kitano, Harry H. L., and Roger Daniels. 1995. *Asian Americans: Emerging Minorities*. Englewood Cliffs, NJ: Prentice Hall.

Kitano, Harry H.L. *Japanese Americans: The Evolution of a Subculture*, 2nd edition, 1976.

Kras, Eva S. 1995. *Management in Two Cultures: Bridging the Gap Between United States and Mexican Managers*. Intercultural Press.

Lach, Jennifer. 1999, February. "The Color of Money". *American Demographics*, 21 (2), 59.

Larson, Wanwadee. 1989. *Confessions of a Mail Order Bride: American Life Through Thai Eyes*. Far Hills, NJ: New Horizon Press.

Levinson, David and Melvin Ember, eds. 1997. *American Immigrant Cultures*. Simon and Schuster Macmillan.

Liedtke, Michael. 2002, May 27. "Banks hope to capture the Hispanic market". *Daily Bulletin*. Retrieved May 29, 2002 from the World Wide Web: http://dailybulletin.com/business/articles/0502/27/biz02.asp.

Lewis, Nantawan Boonprasat. 1997. "Thai" in *American Immigrant Cultures*. Levinson and Ember, eds. Simon and Schuster Macmillan.

"Loose Change". 1997, July. *U.S. Banker*.

Lunt, Penny. 1994, July. "What Asians like and dislike about banks". *ABA Banking Journal* 86(7): 3.

Ma Wong, Angie. 1993. *Target the U.S. Asian Market*. Palos Verdes, CA: Heritage Books.

McKennis, Ann T. 1999. "Caring for the Islamic Patient". *AORN Journal*. 69:6.

McWilliams, Carey. 1964. *Brothers Under the Skin*. Boston, MA: Little, Brown.

Min, P. 1997. "The Korean-American Family" in *Ethnic Families in America: Patterns and Variations*. Mindel, C.H. et al, eds. 4th edition. Englewood Cliffs, NJ: Prentice Hall.

Modell, John. 1968. "The Japanese American Family: A Perspective for Future Investigations". *Pacific Historical Review*. 37.

Mohl, Lucy. 1995. "An Armenian Tapestry". *American Theatre*. 12:7 (Sept).

Morrison, Terri, et al. 1994. *Kiss, Bow, or Shake Hands: How to Do Business in Sixty Countries*. Holbrook, Massachusetts: Adams Media Corporation.

Nakano, Mei T. 1990. *Japanese American Women: Three generations 1890-1990*. Berkeley, CA: Mina Press.

"National Retirement Confidence Survey Results to Be Released". 2001, May 4. *PR Newswire*.

Ogawa, Dennis M. 1971. *From Japs to Japanese*. Berkeley, CA: McCutchan.

Ong, Paul, et al., eds. 1994. *The New Asian Immigration In Los Angeles and Global Restructuring*. Philadelphia: Temple University Press.

Ortiz, Vilma. 1996. "The Mexican-Origin Population: Permanent Working Class or Emerging Middle Class?" in *Ethnic Los Angeles*. Roger Waldinger and Mehdi Bozorgmehr, eds. New York: Russel Sage.

Osako, M.M. 1980. "Aging, Social Isolation and Kinship Ties Among Japanese Americans." *Project Report to the Administration on Aging*.

Oshagan, Emma Papazian. 1996. *Dimensions of Armenian Ethnic Identity as Perceived by Immigrant Armenian Young Male Adults*. Ann Arbor: UMI Dissertation Services.

Pelton, R. et al. 1996. *Fielding's Far East*. Redondo Beach, CA: Fielding Worldwide, Inc.

Pido, Antonio. J. A. 1986. *The Filipinos in America: Macro/Micro Dimensions of Immigration and Integration*. New York: Center for Migration Studies.

Reimers, D. M. 1983 "An Unintended Reform: The 1965 Immigration Act and Third World Immigration to the United States". *Journal of American Ethnic History* 3: 9-28.

Sabagh, Georges and Mehdi Bozorgmehr. "Secular Immigrants: Religiosity and Ethnicity Among Iranian Muslims in Los Angeles", in *Muslim Communities in North America.* Yvonne Yazback Haddad and Jane Idleman Smith, eds. Albany: State University of New York.

Sacks, Karen Brodkin. 1998. "How Jews Became White", in *Race, Class and Gender in the United States: An Integrated Study.* Paula S. Rothenberg, ed. New York: St. Martins Press.

"Salomon Smith Barney Introduces Asian American Investor Education Programs". 2002, May 22. *PR Newswire.*

Schaefer, R. T. 1996. *Racial and Ethnic Groups.* New York: Harper Collins.

Schoenberger, Karl. 1993, October 4. "Breathing Life into Southland". *Los Angeles Times.*

Shaheed, Farida. 1999. "Constructing Identities: Culture, Women's Agency and the Muslim World". *International Social Science Journal.* 51:1.

Sih, P.K. and L.B. Allen. 1976. *The Chinese In America.* New York, New York: St. John's University Press.

"Speaking the Customer's Language—Literally". September 25, 2005. *Business Week.*

Sue, Stanley and Harry Kitano. 1973. "Stereotypes as a Measure of Success." *Journal of Social Issues*: 29, pp. 83-98.

Szanton Blanc, Cristina. 1990 "Collision of Cultures: Historical Reformulations of Gender in the Lowland Visayas, Philippines". In *Power and Difference: Gender in Island Southeast Asia*, edited by J.M. Atkinson and S. Errington. Stanford, California: Stanford University Press.

-----. 1996. "The Thoroughly Modern 'Asian': Culture, Transnationalism, and Nation in Thailand and the Philippines". In *Ungrounded Empires: Cultural Politics in Modern Chinese Transnationalism*, edited by A. Ong and D. Nonnini. New York: Routledge.

-----. 1997. "Filipino" in *American Immigrant Cultures.* Levinson and Ember, eds. Simon and Schuster Macmillan.

Takagi, D.Y.1994. "Japanese American Families", in *Minority Families in the United States: A Multicultural Perspective,* edited by Ronald L. Taylor. Prentice Hall.

Takaki, Ronald. 1989. *Strangers from a Different Shore: A History of Asian Americans.* Boston: Little, Brown.

Talai, V. 1986. "Social Boundaries Within and Between Ethnic Groups: Armenians in London". *Man*, 21: 2 (June).

Tong, Benson. 2000. *The Chinese Americans.* Westport, Connecticut: Greenwood Press.

Tung, May Pao-May. 2000. *Chinese Americans and Their Immigrant Parents.* New York, New York: The Haworth Press, Inc.

Useem, Jerry. 2002. "Banking on Allah". *Fortune,* June 10, 2002, p. 155.

Van Kiem,Thai et al. 1969. *Vietnamese Realities*, 3rd ed. Sai Gon.

Veverka, Amber. 1999, July 13. "Mixing Religion with Investments Doesn't Yield the Best Returns". *Buffalo News*.

Waldinger, Roger and Michael Lichter. 1996. "Anglos: Beyond Ethnicity?" in *Ethnic Los Angeles*. Roger Waldinger and Mehdi Bozorgmehr, eds. New York: Russel Sage.

Wilder Research Center, *Speaking for Themselves: A survey of Hispanic, Hmong, Russian, and Somali immigrants in Minneapolis-Saint Paul* , Wilder Research Center, November 2000 www.wilder.org/research/reports

Yang, Fenggang. 1999. *Chinese Christians in America*. University Park, Pennsylvania: The Pennsylvania State University Press.

Yeretzian, Aram Serkis. 1974. *A History of Armenian Immigration to America With Special Reference to conditions in Los Angeles*. San Francisco: R&E Associates.

Zaretsky, Adam M.1997. "A Burden to America? Immigration and the Economy", *The Regional Economist*. October.

WEB SITES

About.com, The Human Internet: **www.about.com**
AC Nielsen: **www.acnielsen.com**
Africana.com, the Digital Bridge: **www.africana.com**
African American Holiday Association: **www.aaha-info.org**
American Diabetes Association: **www.diabetes.org**
American Heritage Project, A Brief History of Chinese Immigration to America:
    http://www.ailf.org/heritage/chinese/essay01.htm
American Marketing Association: **www.ama.org**
The American Muslim Council: **www.amconline.org**
The Arab American Institute: **www.arab-aai.org**
Arizona State University Hispanic Research Center: **www.asu.edu/clas/hrc**
Armenia Information: **www.aremeniainfo.am**
Asiaco Japan: **www.Japan.asiaco.com/English/**
Asia Source: **www.asiasource.org**

Baylor University: **www.baylor.edu**
The Black Health Network: **www.blackhealthnetwork.com**
B'nai B'rith Interactive: **http://bbi.koz.com/servlet/bbi_ProcServ**

Chinese Culture Center of San Francisco: **www.c-c-c.org**
Chinese Americans: **http://lab2.cc.wmich.edu/mgeasler/fcs568/chinese/**
Chinese American History Timeline: **www.itp.berkeley.edu/~asam121/timeline.html**
Colorado Health Site: **www.coloradohealthnet.org**
Condensed China: **www.asterius.com/china/**
Council on American Islamic Relations: **www.cair-net.org**

Dallas News: Latinos in U.S. grow diverse: **www.dallasnews.com/census/stories.html**
Diversity, Inc.: **www.diversityinc.com**

Embassy of India, Washington, D.C.: **www.indianembassy.org**
Encarta Encyclopedia: **www.encarta.msn.com**
Engaged Buddhist: **www.engagedpage.com**
Explore Japan: **www.explorejapan.com**

Factmonster.com: **www.factmonster.com**
Federal Government of Mexico: **www.presidencia.gob.mx**
Filipino American History: **www.csuchico.edu/ncpaso/filipino.htm**

Goehner.com: "Russian/American cultural contrasts," **www.goehner.com/russinfo.htm**
The Globalist.com: **wysiwyg://24/http://www.theglobalist.com/nor/gdiary/2002/04-01-02.shtml**

History of Korea, University of California, Berkeley: **http://violet.Berkeley.edu/~korea/history.html**

India Network Foundation: **www.indnet.org**
Indian Health Care Beliefs and Practices: **www.baylor.edu/~Charles_Kemp/indian_health.htm**
Indian Visit: **www.indianvisit.com**
Institute of Islamic Information and Education: **www.iiie.net**
Islamic Finance: **www.islamic-finance.net**
Islam Online: **www.islamonline.net**
Islam Questions and Answers: **www.islam-qa.com**
The Islamic Medical Association of North America: **www.imana.org**
IslamiCity: **www.islam.org**
Itihaas Indian History: **www.itihaas.com**

Japanese Americans: **http://lab2.cc.wmich.edu/mgeasler/fcs568/japan/**
Japanese American Citizens League: **www.jacl.org**
Japanese American Internment Camps During WWII, Marriott Library:
　　　　www.lib.utah.edu/spc/photo/9066/9066.htm
The Japanese American Network: **www.janet.org**
Judaism101: **www.jewfaq.org**
The Julian Samora Research Institute: **www.jsri.msu.edu**

Korean American Health Care Beliefs and Practices:
　　　　www.baylor.edu/~Charles_Kemp/asian_health.html
Korean Americans: **www.columbia.edu/itc/sipa/U6210/ik105/history.html**
Korean Americans: **http://lab2.cc.wmich.edu/mgeasler/fcs568/korean/**

Library of Congress Country Studies: **http://lcweb2.loc.gov/frd/cs/**
Little Saigon Television: **www.littlesaigon.com/radio/radio.htm**
Lonely Planet Online: **www.lonelyplanet.com**

Marriage in Korea: **www.sogang.ac.kr/~burns/cult951/marriage.html**
Miami: **www.miami.about.com**
Mongolian Spots: **www.fwcc.org/mongolianspot.htm**
Multicultural Health, University of Michigan: **www.med.umich.edu/1libr/multicul/multi00.htm**
Muslim Student Association: **www.msa-natl.org**
Muslim Women's League: **www.mwlusa.org**

National Council of La Raza: **www.nclr.org**
National Diabetes Clearinghouse: **www.niddk.nih.gov**
National Foundation for Jewish Culture: **www.jewishculture.org**
National Japanese American Historical Society: **www.nikkeiheritage.org**
National Latino Research Center: **www.csusm.edu/nlrc**
Nisei Week Festival: **www.neseiweek.org**

Orange County Asian Pacific Islander Community Alliance: **www.ocapica.org**

Pan American Health Organization, Regional Office for the Americas of the World Health Organization:
   www.paho.org
The Peculiarity of Korean Marriage: **www.sogang.ac.kr/~burns/cult951/marriage.html**
Philippines, WorldRover: **www.worldrover.com/history/philippines_history.html**

Ripnet.org: "Young Russian-American Change 'Old-Believers' "
   www.ripnet.org/triumphant/obchange.htm
Russian Embassy: **www.russianembassy.org**

Saint Barnabas Health Care System, Jewish Genetic Diseases:
   www.sbhcs.com/genetics/offer/index.html
Science News Online: Immigrants Go From Health to Worse:
   www.sciencenews.org/sn_arc98/9_19_98/fob1.htm
Selig Center for Economic Growth: **www.selig.uga.edu**
Strategy Research Corporation: **www.strategyresearch.com**

Thailand: **www.easyholidays.net/thailand/thaifestivals.htm**

UCLA Chicano Studies Research Center: **www.sscnet.ucla.edu/csrc/library**
The Unique Korean Funeral Service: **www.sogang.ac.kr/~burns/cult96/s930056.html**
United States Census: **www.census.gov**
United States Department of Health and Human Services Centers for Disease Control and Prevention:
   www.cdc.gov
United States Department of Health and Human Services National Institutes of Health: **www.nih.gov**

Vietnamese American Council: **www.viet-nam.org**
Vietnamese American Profile: **http://www.baylor.edu/~Charles_Kemp/vietnamese_health.htm**
Vietnamese American Public Affairs Committee: **www.vpac-usa.org**

www.welcome-dominican-republic.com
www.semana-santa.org

Dr. Andrew Erlich

Andrew Erlich, PH.D.

Andrew Erlich, Ph.D. has been generating excitement in the speaking, organizational development, research, motivational analysis and training arenas since 1979. Dr. Erlich designs and conducts keynotes and training sessions that can be presented in both English and Spanish.

His award-winning seminars focus on: Latinos; African Americans; Chinese; Japanese; Filipinos; Koreans; Vietnamese; and Asian Indians.

In addition to compiling *Exploring Culture: How to do Business with 17 Cultural and Religious Groups*, Dr. Erlich is the author of *Selling to Latinos* which is available at **www.andyerlich.com** and **www.etcethnic.com** .